WELSH FARE

S. Minwel Tibbott

WELSH FARE

A Selection of Traditional
Recipes

National Museum of Wales
Welsh Folk Museum
1991

First published: February 1976
Reprinted in 1991

ISBN 0 85485 040 6

© National Museum of Wales (Welsh Folk Museum)

Printed in Wales by D. Brown & Sons Limited,
Cowbridge and Bridgend, Glamorgan

Contents

Acknowledgements

Without the kind co-operation of many persons it would not have been possible to publish this volume. The Welsh Folk Museum wishes to thank these most warmly for their help. Particular mention must be made of the people who provided the information that has been compiled in the text and of others who allowed photographs to be taken for this publication. They are as follows:

Mrs. Mary Barnes, Leasingham, Mrs. Glenys Bebb, Tal-y-llyn, Mrs. Agnes Davies, Llangrannog, Mrs. M. Davies, Llanerfyl, Miss Cissie Davies, Penderyn, Mrs. May Davies, Llan-saint, Mrs. Mary Davies, Llanbryn-Mair, Mrs. Kate Davies, Pren-gwyn, Mrs. Hannah Davies, Llandysul, Mrs. Hannah Mary Davies, Brynberian, Mrs. Gwen Davies, Dowlais, Commander John Penry Davies, Cricieth, Mrs. May Edwards, Abercywarch, Mrs. Annie Davies-Evans, Ystalyfera, Mrs. Mary Evans, Rhyd-y-main, Dolgellau, Miss Mary Evans, Mynytho, Mrs. Catrin Evans, Cynllwyd, Mrs. Elizabeth Evans, Llanwrda, Mrs. Jane Evans, Cellan, Mrs. Myra Evans, Gilfachreda, Mr. and Mrs. Evans, Llanrhystud, Miss Sarah Aerona Griffiths, Aber-porth, Mrs. S. A. Griffiths, Gwaelod-y-garth, Mrs. Alice Hughes, Denbigh, Mrs. Elizabeth Hughes, Garn Fadrun, Misses Myfanwy and Sally Hughes, Blaenau Ffestiniog, Mrs. E. James, Llanarthney, Mrs. Violet James, Hebron, Mrs. Mary Jane Jenkins, Sarnau, Mrs. Pattie John, Mynachlog-ddu, Mrs. Ann Jones, Ciliau Aeron, Mrs. Annie Jones, Farmers, Mrs. Catrin Jones, Bala, Mrs. Elizabeth Jones, Nefyn, Miss Margied Jones, Llanuwchllyn, Mrs. Margaret E. Jones, Lleyn, Mrs. Gwenllian Jones, Whitchurch, Cardiff, Mrs. Rosalie Jones, Whitchurch, Cardiff, Mrs. H. Jones, Llangadfan,

Miss Margretta Jones, Parc, Mrs. Nellie Jones, Uwchmynydd, Mr. and Mrs. William Jones, Cenarth, Miss Ann Llywelyn, Garnant, Mrs. Margaret Maddocks, North Cornelly, Mrs. Ann Mainwaring, Port Talbot, Miss N. Millward, Gwaelod-y-garth, Mrs. Margaret Morgan, Pont-y-clun, Miss Rachel Morgan, Tre-lech, Mr. and Mrs. Tom Morgans, Cwm-bach, Mrs. Ann Elin Morris, Parc, Mrs. Gwen Owens, Fach-wen, Miss Eluned Phillips, Cenarth, Mrs. Margaret Phillips, Roath, Cardiff, Mrs. A. Powell, Heolsenni, Mrs. Olivia Preece, Port Talbot, Miss Laura Pugh, Cricieth, Mrs. Margaret Rees, Groes-goch, Mrs. Mary Rees, Roath, Cardiff, Mrs. Elizabeth Reynolds, Brynhoffnant, Mrs. Margaret G. Roberts, Kenfig Hill, Dr. Kate Roberts, Denbigh, Mr. I. H. Roberts, Llanfachraeth, Mr. I. E. Rowlands, Holyhead, Mrs. Olwen Samuel, Ebbw Vale, Mrs. Margretta Thomas, Nantgarw, Mrs. Elizabeth Thomas, Croes-lan, Miss Mati Thomas, Rhydlewis, Mrs. Mary Thomas, Pen-prysg, Pen-coed, Miss Jennie Thomas, Pen-tyrch, Mrs. Rachel Thomas, Manordeilo, Mrs. Elizabeth Anne Thomas, Newport, Pembrokeshire, Mrs. G. Megan Tibbott, Aberystwyth, Mrs. G. Tucker, Gower Peninsula, Mrs. Gladys Elizabeth Walters, Llangynydd, Misses Annie and Rachel Williams, Aberdaron, Mrs. Elin Lloyd Williams, Bryngwran, Mrs. Elizabeth Williams, Cwmaman, Aberdare, Mrs. Margaret Ann Williams, Aberdare, Mr. D. I. Williams, Crug-y-bar, Mrs. Annie Williams, Pwllheli, Mr. John Williams, Llangwnadl, 'Pensiwnydd' from Anglesey.

7

Foreword

The main task of the Welsh Folk Museum since it opened in 1948 has been to collect and record, to study and reflect the folk life of Wales in all its various forms. The advent of the tape recorder made it possible to record the voice of informants and also facilitated the building of a comprehensive account of the traditional life of our country by the Department of Oral Traditions and Dialects. It is the responsibility of the Welsh Folk Museum, having collected this oral evidence from the oldest inhabitants with their generous cooperation, not only to preserve this historical information for the benefit of future scholars, but to present it, where appropriate, to contemporary readers as part of their inheritance. This volume, based on the collection of recordings in the Welsh language, made by members of the Department of Oral Traditions and Dialects over the last few years, is a forerunner of a number of similar volumes which it is hoped to publish. It was prepared by Mrs. S. Minwel Tibbott, an Assistant Keeper in that Department, and is based on evidence which she collected from a large number of speakers throughout Wales who readily supplied information concerning traditional dishes. I have pleasure in acknowledging the invaluable assistance of these friends whose names are listed on another page. I should also like to thank the Editor of Y Cymro, a Welsh language newspaper, for permission to publish the recipes on page 29 and the photograph on page 68, the Editor of the Western Mail for permitting the publication of some of the recipes on pages 21, 27, 34, 35, 39, 40, 41, 42, 43, 49, 50 and 64, and to Miss Margaret Brentnall, Highgate, London, for allowing us to publish the photograph on page 67. The other photographs were taken by members of the Welsh Folk Museum staff.

The format and design of the volume was undertaken by the Welsh Books Council, and I should like to thank the Council and its Director, Mr. Alun Creunant Davies, who gave us valuable advice regarding the problems of printing. We are also indebted to the Head of the Council's Design Department, Mr. Elgan Davies, for his untiring work in presenting the forerunner of this volume for publication in the Welsh language. The present volume is an English edition of that work under the title *Amser Bwyd* first published in February 1974.

November 1975

Trefor M. Owen, Curator,
Welsh Folk Museum

Introduction

Food and drink form an important part of a nation's heritage, and the need to retain information about the dishes that were once synonymous with the Welsh way of life instigated the compiling of this volume.

First and foremost it is a selection of recipes, but the notes accompanying a large number of them will give the reader a brief insight into their historical background. Indeed, the inclusion of any or every one of these dishes in the collection shows that they have played a specific role in the history of food in Wales.

It would be difficult to assign these foods to specific periods. We know that they were prepared extensively at the turn of the twentieth century, a period that is vividly remembered by the majority of the older inhabitants of Wales today. Their knowledge of them, backed by years of practical experience, has provided us with the main information compiled in this volume. This information is now being kept in the archives of the Welsh Folk Museum either in the form of interview recorded on tape, or in manuscript. A recipe may well be compared with a folk song or folk tale; all three are transferred orally from person to person, from generation to generation, and their preservation depends entirely on the strength or weakness of the human memory. Slight modifications are inevitable over a period of years. A slip of the memory or the wish to improvise may well account for the minor variations discernible when more than one recipe is given for a particular dish. Local customs attached to many of the dishes are evident too.

The general character of a nation's cuisine is determined to a very great extent by the country's products which are in turn the result of its physical environment. Oats, the main cereal crop grown in Wales, and bacon, which has been an important part of the staple diet of rural Wales in the past, have prominent places in this collection, augmented by root crops, garden vegetables and dairy products. Salted beef, mutton, fish and poultry are also featured. Governed by these readily-available raw materials most of the traditional dishes may be described as plain, wholesome foods, but the preparing and cooking of them without present-day facilities demanded great skill. Photographs have been included to illustrate the traditional methods of cooking many of them.

It was not intended to include every recognized dish nor to represent every district throughout Wales in this one volume. The aim is to re-introduce a selection of traditional Welsh foods to the people of Wales today. The majority of them will most certainly find their way back to present-day menus, but the remaining few—the less palatable ones perhaps—have been included on the merit of their historical significance. Older readers may find obvious gaps in the collection and they are invited to forward any relevant information to the Welsh Folk Museum, St Fagans', Cardiff.

Boiling toffee in a copper pan. Kennixton, Welsh Folk Museum. ➤

Savoury Dishes

Cawl Cig Mochyn a Chig Eidion— Bacon and Beef Broth

one joint each of bacon and beef
carrots
swede
cabbage
potatoes
leeks
parsley
oatmeal
water

(Salted meat should be allowed to stand in cold water overnight to remove excess salt.)
Put the meat joints in a large saucepan, cover with water and boil for an hour or more. Then add the carrots, swede and cabbage, all coarsely cut. (Leaves of nettles and savoury may be added in the spring when green vegetables are scarce.) Boil for another fifteen minutes before adding the potatoes. Continue to cook and then add the leeks and parsley, finely chopped, within ten minutes of serving. (The meat joints may be lifted out of the broth before adding the leeks and parsley.) Finally, thicken the broth with a tablespoonful of oatmeal (or plain flour) mixed with a little cold water.
Serve the broth clear, with small pieces of bread, in basins or bowls. Serve the vegetables with slices of meat as a second course.
Pren-gwyn, Cardiganshire

Bacon broth (without beef) was prepared in the same way.
Brynberian, Pembrokeshire.

Cawl (broth) was the dish most commonly served for dinner on the farm during the winter months and it was regarded as a very nutritious meal. It was served in wooden bowls and eaten with wooden spoons. Apple dumplings and oatmeal trollies were sometimes boiled in the broth along with the meat and vegetables. (see respective recipes.)
Pren-gwyn, Cardiganshire.

Cawl Awst was the best broth of the year when a wide variety of fresh garden vegetables were available. A feast known as *Cawl Awst* was held, primarily for sailors, on New Quay beach on the first day of August. The broth, boiled in a large cauldron, would be prepared under the supervision of one woman and most families in the neighbourhood would supply the required meat (fresh beef occasionally) and vegetables.
New Quay, Cardiganshire.

Cawl ffwt a berw. This particular name was given to the broth that was prepared rather hurriedly by cutting the meat and vegetables into small pieces and boiling them all together until they were cooked.
Tre-lech, Carmarthenshire.

Cawl pen lletwad was the name given to a vegetable broth prepared only when meat was in short supply.
Cwm-bach, Carmarthenshire.

Cawl twymo. It was generally the custom to reheat the broth that was left over from the mid-day meal and to serve it for supper on the same day, or for lunch on the following day.
Pren-gwyn, Cardiganshire.

Cawl Pys—Pea Broth

a piece of stewing beef (shin)
ham bone
split-peas
parsnips
carrots
swede
onions
potatoes
water
plain white flour

Soak the split-peas in cold water for an hour or two, or overnight. Cover the meat with cold water in a saucepan, bring to the boil, then change the water. Boil the meat for an hour or more before adding the split-peas. Continue boiling for a few minutes and then add the coarsely chopped carrots, parsnips and swede. (The quantities will vary according to size of saucepan and personal taste.) Allow the broth to simmer for a short time again before adding the potatoes. Then boil for a further twenty minutes. Finally, mix a little plain flour in cold water and add it gradually to the broth to thicken it. (It is advisable to lift the meat out of the broth before thickening it.)
Dowlais, Glamorgan.

This broth was served in large soup-plates in the miners' homes in south Wales, and was regarded as one of their favourite evening meals during the winter months.

Cawl Cennin a Phersli—Leek and Parsley Broth

a piece of stewing beef (shin)
best end of a neck of lamb
carrots
parsnips
swede
small onions
potatoes
leeks and parsley
water
flour

Cover the meat with salt water in a large saucepan, bring to the boil and simmer for an hour or more. Cut the carrots and parsnips lengthwise and the swede into fairly small pieces, then add to the meat and water.

(Quantities will vary according to personal taste etc.) Boil the broth for a further few minutes before adding the potatoes and the finely chopped leeks. A little more water may be added at this stage, if needed.
Continue cooking for another twenty minutes and then thicken with a thin paste of flour and water. Finally, add the finely chopped parsley and re-boil for a few minutes only before serving.
Serve the broth itself with a little bread. The meat, potatoes and vegetables may be served as a second course.
Dowlais, Glamorgan.

Leek and parsley broth was one of the dishes prepared for the miners' evening meal in south Wales.

Lobsgows—Lobscouse

a piece of salted beef
cold water
a large onion
carrots
swede
potatoes

Using a large saucepan, cover the meat with water and boil for some time before adding the chopped onion, swede and carrots. (Alternatively, dice the meat and boil for a shorter period, as time permits.) Continue cooking and finally add the potatoes some twenty minutes before serving.
(The quantity of potatoes and vegetables added will determine the final thickness of the broth.)
Mynytho, Lleyn.

Lobsgows was commonly eaten for the mid-day meal on the farms in the counties of north Wales or for *swper chwarel* (evening meal) in the slate-mining communities there.
Mynytho, Lleyn and Rhostryfan, Caernarvonshire.

Cawl Coch Ysgyfarnog—Hare Broth

one hare
carrots
potatoes
leeks and parsley
salt to taste
one tablespoonful oatmeal
cold water

Skin, clean and halve the hare and soak overnight in cold, salt water.

Using a large, heavy saucepan, cover the hare and the finely sliced carrots with cold water and bring to the boil. Then add the leeks and parsley, finely chopped, and the salt. Mix the oatmeal with a little cold water, add to the broth and boil until the meat is tender and falling off the bone. Lift the meat out of the broth before adding the potatoes and then boil for a further twenty minutes. Serve the meat, potatoes and vegetables with the broth.
Rhydlewis, Cardiganshire.

Potes Cig—Meat Broth

one joint each of salted beef and bacon
carrots
cabbage
swede
potatoes
water

Put the meat and the vegetables, finely chopped, in a large saucepan, cover with water and boil until the meat is fairly tender. Then add the potatoes, cut in halves, and boil for a further twenty minutes.
On the farms the meat, potatoes and vegetables were served for the mid-day meal, but it was general custom to keep the broth for breakfast on the following day. It was re-heated and poured over small pieces of bread or crushed oatcake to make a dish known as *brwes*.
Parc, Bala, Merioneth.

Potes Cig Pen Oen ac Iau— Lamb's Head and Liver Broth

lamb's head
liver
water
onions
salt

Stand the head and liver overnight in salt water, then wash and clean thoroughly.
Boil the head, liver and onions together until the meat falls off the bone. Lift the head and liver out of the broth, remove all the meat from the bones, dice both the meat and liver into small cubes (approximately a quarter of an inch thick) and return into the broth.

Serve immediately.
Rhostryfan, Caernarvonshire.

This particular dish was known as *pinshons* in the slate quarrying district of Bethel, Caernarvonshire, and was served with mashed potatoes for *swper chwarel* (the evening meal).

Cosyn Pen—Brawn

a pig's head, kidneys and tongue
a joint of beef
water
pepper and salt

Clean the head, remove the eyes and cut off the ears. Split into easily managed pieces and stand in brine for three or four days.
Wash the pieces thoroughly before putting them into a large saucepan, together with the tongue, kidneys and beef joint. Boil for three hours or until the meat falls off

Boiling a pig's head to make brawn. Abercywarch, Merioneth.

the bone. Lift all the pieces on to a large plate, remove all meat from the bone and place on a large open dish. Using a sharp knife chop finely. Season well, mix thoroughly and put in an earthenware dish to cool and set. Alternatively put the mixture in a colander, cover with a plate and press it with a heavy weight to remove excess fat.
Slice when cold and serve.
Tonyrefail, Glamorgan.

Keep the tongue whole after boiling, remove skin and sandwich it between two layers of the seasoned minced meat.
Press together and slice when cold.
Dowlais, Glamorgan.

Faggots

pig's liver
breadcrumbs from half a stale loaf
one pound onions
salt and pepper
a little sage
a pig's flead

Mince the liver very finely with a sharp knife on a wooden board and put in an earthenware bowl. (A metal mincer tends to give the liver a bitter taste.) Add the onions, peeled and finely chopped, and the breadcrumbs, season and mix well with a wooden spoon. Spread the flead on a wooden board and cut into pieces of four to six inches square. (The flead will stretch and become more supple by soaking in tepid water before cutting.) Wrap each piece of flead around about a tablespoonful of the mixture to form a faggot. Place these side by side in a large roasting tin and cook in a moderately hot oven.
Serve warm with peas and gravy.
Tonyrefail, Glamorgan.

Preparing and cooking the faggots on the morning when the butcher returned to cut up the pig was a ritual in the Tonyrefail district so that he and his helpers could partake of them during the mid-day meal.

Faggots

pig's liver
three onions
one teaspoonful chopped sage
salt and pepper
small pieces of pork fat
a pig's flead

Soak the liver in boiling water for a few minutes before slicing. Mince the liver, onions and pork fat and put in a large bowl. (The pork fat helps to keep the faggots moist.) Mix the ingredients well and season with salt, pepper and sage. Cut the flead into pieces of about six inches square, wrap each piece around a little of the mixture and place the faggots in rows, in a meat tin. Cook in a moderately hot oven.
Upper Banwy, Montgomery.

A pig's flead. Mrs. May Edwards, Abercywarch, Merioneth.

A 'flat hearth' at Pontfaen, Ciliau Aeron, Cardiganshire.>

Bola Mochyn—Tripe

After killing a pig, clean the tripe immediately under cold running water. Allow to stand in salt water and lime for nine days, changing the liquid daily. Then wash it thoroughly before putting it in a large saucepan. Cover with water and boil until tender. Lift it out on to a large dish and press. When set, cut into slices and fry in bacon fat with onions.
Kenfig Hill, Glamorgan.

Pwdin Gwaed—Black Pudding

the pig's blood on day of killing
one pint cold water
a little salt
onions
mixed herbs
a little oatmeal
pig's small intestine
a little fat off the small intestine

Pour the blood into a large bowl while warm and stir constantly until cold to avoid clotting. Then dilute with a pint of water, add a little salt and allow to stand overnight.

Wash the intestine thoroughly, inside and out, and put in salt water overnight.

Chop the onions, coat them and the pieces of fat with oatmeal, season with herbs and stir into the blood. Work this mixture into the small intestine, secure with string at both ends, allowing for expansion during boiling. Boil the pudding in water for about half an hour and then hang to dry in a suitable place.
Slice, when needed, and fry with bacon.
Nantgarw, Glamorgan.

Cig Moch a Chabaits—Bacon and Cabbage

bacon or ham joint
cabbage
potatoes
parsley

Stand the meat in cold water overnight to remove excess salt. Boil the meat until tender and keep the stock. Cook the cabbage in this stock and then drain. Boil the potatoes in another saucepan and again keep the water.

Parsley Sauce
To the potato water, add a little milk, butter and chopped parsley. Thicken with a little flour mixed with cold water and boil for a few minutes. Serve with the boiled potatoes, cabbage and cold sliced bacon.
Ystalyfera, Glamorgan.

Cig moch a chabaits was another popular dish prepared for the miner's evening meal in south Wales.

Cig Moch a Chaws a Winwns— Bacon, Cheese and Onions

bacon rashers
cheese
onions, chopped
salt and pepper

Place bacon rashers on an enamel or an oven-proof plate, cover with fairly thick slices of cheese and top with a thick layer of chopped onion. Cover with another plate and bake in a slow oven.
Ystalyfera, Glamorgan.

Cig Moch, Iau a Nionod— Liver, Bacon and Onions

half a pound bacon rashers
one pound liver
onions
salt and pepper
a little plain flour

Slice the liver and toss in seasoned flour.
Fry the bacon rashers lightly and lift out on to a warm dish. Fry the liver and chopped onion in the bacon fat and then place with the bacon. Make gravy by mixing a tablespoonful of plain flour into the fat in the pan,

adding a little boiling water and stir well. Boil for a few minutes.
Serve this dish with boiled potatoes.
Lleyn, Caernarvonshire.

This particular dish was served for *swper chwarel* in the slate quarrying districts of north Wales.
Rhostryfan, Caernarvonshire.

Cig Mochyn wedi'i Ferwi—Boiled Ham

ham joint
water
demerara sugar

Cover the ham joint with water and boil, allowing fifteen minutes for every pound and an extra fifteen minutes. Using a sharp knife, remove the rind, coat the joint with demerara sugar and melt it over the meat.
Rolling a clean red-hot poker over the sugared joint was common practice at one time, but alternatively the joint may be placed under a hot grill or in a hot oven for a few minutes.
Llanarthney, Carmarthenshire.

Tato Rhost—Roast Potatoes

potatoes
bacon rashers
onions or chives
a little water

Place three or four bacon rashers in a saucepan, cover with alternate layers of potatoes and sliced onions and finally place bacon rashers on top.
Simmer slowly in a little water until the potatoes have finally absorbed the water and have subsequently browned in the bacon fat.
Pren-gwyn, Cardiganshire.

This meal was cooked without much supervision in a *ffwrn fach* (pot oven), suspended over an open fire. Hence *tato rhost a llaeth enwyn* (*tato rhost* and buttermilk) was a meal popularly served on the farms on churning day.
Tato pobi was the name given to this dish in another part of Cardiganshire, e.g.
Cellan, Cardiganshire.

Cig ar wyneb tato This meal resembles *tato rhost* but is prepared in a slightly different way:
Par-boil the potatoes in a heavy saucepan and then cover with bacon rashers. Finally, top with a thick layer of chopped onions or chives. Cover with a closely fitting lid and continue cooking in very little water for about half an hour. The bacon fat will seep through and brown the potatoes at the bottom of the pan.
Crug-y-bar, Carmarthenshire.

Tatws Pum Munud—A Five Minute Dish

bacon rashers
potatoes
onions
salt and pepper
a little flour
water

Fry the bacon rashers in a deep frying pan and then lift on to a plate. Slice the potatoes and onions and fry in the bacon fat. Season well and sprinkle with a little flour. Then add water so that the potatoes are barely covered and lay the bacon rashers on top. Cook slowly until the water is absorbed and the potatoes turn golden brown.

A dish served for the mid-day meal.
Mynytho, Lleyn.

Tatws Popty—Roast Potatoes

joint of fresh meat (preferably beef)
potatoes
onions
water

Roast the meat in a large tin for an hour or longer. Arrange the potatoes (cut in halves) and the onions (finely chopped) around the meat and pour a little boiling water over them. Cover the tin with a lid and roast until the meat is cooked and the potatoes are browned.
Mynytho, Lleyn.

An alternative method of cooking the same dish is as follows:
Place a thick layer of potatoes and onions on the bottom of a large meat tin and cover with water. Place the joint on top and roast in a hot oven.

This meal was served on special occasions, e.g. on corn-threshing day on the farms.
Garnfadrun, Lleyn.

Tatws Stêm—Steamed Potatoes

potatoes, coarsely cut
onions
bacon rashers
a little flour
water

Fill a saucepan with alternate layers of potatoes and sliced onions, finishing with a layer of potatoes. Sprinkle with a little flour and cover with bacon rashers. Add water to the level of the last layer of potatoes, cover the bacon with grease-proof paper and press firmly with a plate. Place a lid on the saucepan and simmer the contents until cooked.

A favourite dish served for dinner or supper in Porth Dinllaen.
Nefyn, Lleyn.

Mwtrin—Mashed Potatoes

potatoes
swede, dried peas or carrots
salt

Peel and wash the vegetables, as required, and cut into coarse pieces. (Allow the peas to soak overnight.) Par-boil the swede, peas or carrots in salt water before adding the potatoes. Continue boiling for a further fifteen minutes until cooked. Drain and mash until smooth.
Serve with fried bacon.

This meal was generally served at mid-day.
Mynytho, Lleyn.

Stwnsh is an alternative name for the same dish in other areas in north Wales; swedes, peas or carrots would be mashed with the potatoes and consequently given the name *stwnsh rwdan* (swede), *stwnsh pys* (peas) or *stwnsh moron* (carrots).

A specially carved wooden tool was used to mash the vegetables and was known as *mopren, pwnner, stwnsher* or *mutrwr tatws* in different parts of the country.

Tatws yn eu Crwyn—
Potatoes in their Jackets

Scrub the potatoes clean, and bake in a hot oven. Split open, sprinkle with salt and dot with butter. Serve while warm.
Y Fach-wen, Caernarvonshire.

A simple method, practised in many districts, was to place the potatoes between the front bars of the grate and bake them in the glow of the bright, clean fire.
Dyffryn Ardudwy, Merioneth.

Tatws Llaeth—Potatoes with Buttermilk

Wash the potatoes thoroughly and boil in their jackets. Peel off the skin and serve in individual bowls or basins. Add buttermilk and eat while warm.
Dyffryn Ardudwy, Merioneth.

Tatws Menyn—Potatoes with Butter

Boil potatoes in their jackets and then peel off the skin. Put into individual bowls or basins, add butter and mix well into the potatoes. Serve immediately.
Rhostryfan, Caernarvonshire.

Tatws wedi'u Berwi—Boiled Potatoes

Wash and peel the potatoes, and boil in the usual way. Drain, mash and serve with meat or as a snack with buttermilk. *Stwmp, bwts, potsh* and *ponshin* are names given to this dish in different areas.

Tatws Popty—Roast Potatoes

After roasting a joint of meat, lift it out of the tin, and
pour away all excess fat.
Fill the tin with potatoes, sliced thickly, lengthways, and
cover with a layer of finely chopped onion. Sprinkle with
a little salt, pepper and flour and cover with boiling water.
Roast in a hot oven until the potatoes are golden brown.

A meal prepared for *swper chwarel* (the evening meal)
in the slate-quarrying districts of north Wales.
Y Fach-wen, Caernarvonshire.

Pastai Neithior—Bidding Pie

twelve ounces plain flour
five ounces lard
half a pound mutton, boiled, boned and diced
an onion, chopped finely
one teaspoonful salt
one teaspoonful mixed herbs
a little water
a little mutton stock

Sift the flour and salt into a large bowl. Melt the lard
slowly in a little water, bring to the boil and immediately
pour into the flour. Work the melted lard into the flour
and knead well to a soft dough. Turn out on to a floured
board and roll out fairly thinly. Grease a pie dish and
line it with the pastry.
Fill with the mutton and onion, add the seasoning and
stock. Cover with a second layer of pastry, pressing the
edges of both layers together to seal. Cut a slit in the
centre and cook in a moderately hot oven for about
an hour.

When 'bidding weddings' were celebrated on the Gower
peninsula, this pie was specially prepared for the wedding
feast held at the bride's home. A local farmer would
supply the meat by killing a sheep for the occasion and
the womenfolk would join forces to prepare and cook the
pies. The pie was served cold with beer.
A certain person was appointed by the bride's family to
invite their relatives and friends to attend the feast.
He was known as *gwahoddwr* (bidder), and during the
feast he was also given the all important task of
recording the actual sum of money paid by each guest for
a small piece of pie—the sum would vary between five
and ten shillings. The young couple were partly
dependent on this gift-money to set up home. In turn,
they would be invited to similar feasts, and would be
expected to re-pay their 'debt' to the bride' and groom's
families.
Gower Peninsula.

Pastai Persli—Parsley Pie

short-crust pastry
two eggs
half a pint milk
one dessertspoonful plain flour
a little salt
two tablespoonfuls sugar
one dessertspoonful chopped parsley
one and a half ounces fat bacon, diced

Line a deep pie dish thinly with the prepared pastry.
Mix the flour with a little of the milk. Beat the eggs in
a large basin, pour in the remainder of the milk and
add the blended milk and flour, salt, sugar and parsley.
Mix well and pour on to the pastry. Finally, add the bacon
and bake in a fairly hot oven for half an hour or until the
mixture has set.

This pie was usually eaten cold for afternoon tea.
Gower Peninsula.

Pastai Preseli—Preseli Pie

one pound mashed potatoes
two ounces bacon
two ounces cooked lean meat
one onion, chopped finely
a little chopped sage
salt and pepper
short-crust pastry

Cut the bacon into small pieces and fry lightly. Add the
chopped onion and fry together for a few minutes. Add
the diced cooked meat and the sage and heat thoroughly
for a further few minutes before mixing with the mashed
potatoes. Season with salt and pepper.

Line a pie dish with the pastry and bake blind in a hot oven. Fill the pastry case with the prepared mixture and bake in a hot oven for about ten minutes until the top is golden brown.
Serve the pie while hot with gravy.
Pembrokeshire.

Pastai Morgannwg—Glamorgan Pie

one pint milk
two eggs
one and a half ounces flour
a little salt
three ounces bacon, diced
two tablespoonfuls chopped parsley
a little chopped chives
short-crust pastry

Line a pie dish with the pastry. Mix the flour with a little of the milk. Bring the remainder to boiling point, add the blended milk and flour, and bring to the boil again, stirring continuously for about two minutes.
Allow this mixture to cool and then add the eggs, well beaten, and the other ingredients. Mix well, pour on to the pastry and bake in a moderately hot oven for about an hour.
Llanover, Monmouthshire.

Dowset—Bacon Pie

bacon, cut into small pieces
one onion, chopped
a little butter
salt and pepper
short-crust pastry

Line a large oven-proof plate with a thin layer of pastry. Spread the bacon pieces and chopped onion thickly over the pastry, season with salt and pepper and dot with butter. Cover with a second layer of pastry, and seal. Bake in a moderately hot oven.
Gower Peninsula.

Pwdin Pys—Pease Pudding

half a pound split peas
one egg, well beaten
a little butter and sugar
salt and pepper

Wash the peas thoroughly and soak in cold water overnight. Put the peas in a muslin bag, tie securely, but allow for expansion. Put the bag in a saucepan, cover with boiling water, and add a little salt. Boil briskly for about two hours or until the peas are soft. Lift the bag out of the water and drain. Take the peas out of the bag and work them through a fine sieve or colander into a large dish. Add the butter, the egg, salt, pepper and sugar. Beat well for a few minutes until thoroughly mixed. Place the mixture on a floured cloth, roll up and tie both ends securely. Boil the pudding for another half an hour. Turn out on to a hot dish, slice and serve with salt beef or pork.
Gower Peninsula.

Cwningen mewn Corbys—Rabbit in Lentils

a rabbit
one cupful stock
a little parsley, thyme and bay leaf
a little bacon, diced
bacon dripping
cooked lentils

Wash the skinned rabbit thoroughly, joint and fry in a little dripping. When lightly browned, add the bacon and stock, and season with the parsley, thyme and bay leaf. Cover the frying pan and simmer slowly until cooked. Meanwhile, pass the cooked lentils and the liquid in which they were boiled through a sieve into a saucepan. Add to this purée any liquid that remains in the frying pan after removing the meat, etc. Boil the purée briskly until it is reduced to a thick gravy. Pour over the rabbit joints and serve with potatoes and swede.
Gower Peninsula.

Stiw Cwningen—Rabbit Stew

a rabbit, skinned and cleaned
half a pound bacon
swede
carrots
one ounce flour
two or three onions
a little chopped parsley
a little fat
salt and pepper

Joint the rabbit and coarsely cut the bacon and the vegetables. Put all the prepared ingredients in a large saucepan, season with salt, pepper and parsley, cover with water and simmer slowly for about an hour and a half. Lastly, thicken with the flour mixed with a little cold water, and re-boil for a further few minutes.
Lleyn, Caernarvonshire.

Pwdin Gwaed Gwyddau— Goose-blood Pudding

blood from a number of geese
one or two tablespoonfuls oatmeal
plain flour
salt and pepper
sugar
onion, chopped finely

Keep the blood from a number of geese (when killing them for the Christmas market) and beat well with a fork until cold, to avoid lumps forming. Mix the oatmeal and flour with a small quantity of the blood and add to the remainder. Season with pepper, salt and sugar and fold in the chopped onion. Remove the skin from a goose's neck and sew to form a long bag. Pour the blood mixture into it and secure tightly at both ends. Immerse in boiling water and boil for two to three hours. Slice when cold and fry in bacon fat.

This 'pudding' was served with potatoes or with bread and butter.
Llangybi, Caernarvonshire.

Pwdin Rhynion—Groats Pudding

oat groats
water
black treacle

Boil a few cupfuls of groats in water with a little black treacle. When soft, drain the groats, and pour into a large dish. Add more treacle, to taste, whilst warm.

A traditional dish served with goose for Christmas dinner.
Rhyd-y-main, Merioneth.

Troliod—Trollies

oatmeal or plain flour
currants (if desired)
a little broth

When boiling broth, skim a little of the surface fat and put it in a bowl together with some oatmeal or flour. Mix with a little broth to make a soft dough. Add a few currants, if desired.
Divide the dough into equal parts and form into small balls. Immerse in the boiling broth and cook with the mixed vegetables for a few minutes.
Serve with the meat and vegetables.
Pren-gwyn, Cardiganshire.

The trollies were prepared as a substitute for potatoes when these were in short supply in early spring.
Cwm-bach, Carmarthenshire.

Ponco—Omelette

two eggs
a little milk
a little flour

Add the milk to the well-beaten eggs and pour gradually into the flour. Beat well to form a light, smooth batter. Heat a little bacon fat in the frying pan and pour the batter into it. Cook until golden brown on both sides. Serve with fried bacon.
Nefyn, Lleyn.

Eggs would not be included in the batter when they were in short supply; flour and milk or water would be the only ingredients used.
Dyffryn Ardudwy, Merioneth.

Caws wedi'i Bobi—Welsh Rarebit

cheese
a slice of bread

Toast a slice of bread. Bake a large slice of cheese and place on top of the toast.

Slices of home-made cheese were baked in front of an open fire either by holding it on the tip of a toasting fork or by placing it on a plate on an iron stand.
Banwy Uchaf, Montgomeryshire.

A hot grill is the obvious substitute for the open fire in this instance.

Caws a Chwrw—Cheese and Beer

cheese
milk
beer
salt and pepper
a slice of bread (toasted)

Put a large piece of cheese in a saucepan, add a little milk and beer. Season with salt and pepper. Slowly mix the melting cheese with the milk and beer, and bring to the boil. Pour over the toast and serve while warm.
Dyffryn Ardudwy, Merioneth.

Griddle Cakes

Teisennau Crwn—Round Cakes

one pound self-raising flour
four ounces butter
four ounces lard
four ounces currants
four ounces sugar
a little nutmeg
quarter teaspoonful salt
one egg
a little milk

Rub the butter and lard into the flour and then add all the
other dry ingredients. Mix together well.
Beat the egg, add a little milk to it and gradually pour into
the dry ingredients. Knead well to make a light, soft
dough. Turn out on to a floured board, roll out to a
thickness of about a quarter of an inch and cut into
small rounds.
To bake them by means of radiated heat (see note on use
of the Dutch oven) put the cakes in a shallow tin and
bake in a low position under a hot grill. Bake on both
sides until golden brown.
North Cornelly, Glamorgan.

It is certain that the cakes, generally known today as
'Welsh Cakes', have been tea-time favourites in
Glamorgan since the latter decades of the last century.
At one period they would be eaten regularly in
farmhouses and cottages alike, and the miner would also
expect to find them in his food-box. Two different
methods of baking these cakes were practised in
Glamorgan. Baking them on a bakestone over an open
fire may be regarded as the most general practice
throughout the county. The Welsh names given to the
cakes were usually based on the Welsh name for the
bakestone, and these included *pice ar y mân, tishan ar y
mân* and *tishen lechwan.* They varied in size from small,
round cakes to a single cake as big as the bakestone.
The method favoured in the Vale of Glamorgan, on the
other hand, was to bake them in a Dutch oven in front of
an open fire. The cakes were cut into small rounds,
placed in two or three rows on the bottom of the oven
and baked in front of a clean, red glow. These were
known as *pica/pice bach, tishan gron,* and *tishen rown.*
Slashers and *tishan whîls* were colloquial names given
to them in two small villages.

Pica Bach—Bakestone Cakes

eight ounces self-raising flour
four ounces butter
four ounces sugar
one ounce currants
a little salt
half a teaspoonful mixed spice
one egg, well beaten

Sift together the flour, salt and spice, rub in the butter
and finally add the sugar. Mix in the beaten egg and
knead to a fairly dry, soft dough. Halve the dough and
work the currants into one half only. Roll out both halves
of the dough separately to a thickness of about a quarter

24

*Baking round cakes in a Dutch oven. Mrs. Margaret Maddocks,
North Cornelly, Glamorgan.>*

of an inch and cut into small rounds. Bake on a lightly greased bakestone over a moderate heat allowing about two minutes for each side.

Split open the plain cakes and spread with jam, if desired, and serve warm. Alternatively, roll out the plain dough into one large round, bake on both sides on a bakestone, then split open and spread one half with stewed apple and brown sugar. Cover with the other half, sprinkle with sugar and cut into small squares.
Pont-y-clun, Glamorgan.

Welsh Cakes

one pound plain flour
six ounces lard
half a teaspoonful salt
one cupful sugar
one cupful currants
half a teaspoonful bicarbonate of soda
half a pint sour buttermilk

Rub the lard into the flour and add all the other dry ingredients. Dissolve the bicarbonate of soda in the sour buttermilk and work into the dry ingredients to make a soft dough. Turn out on to a floured board, roll out until it is about a quarter of an inch thick and cut into small rounds.

Bake both sides on a very lightly greased bakestone over a moderate heat.
Pennant, Montgomeryshire.

Cacen Gri—Griddle Cake

half a pound flour
four ounces butter
two ounces sugar
one egg, well beaten
two ounces currants
quarter teaspoonful salt
half teaspoonful bicarbonate of soda
buttermilk or milk

Rub the butter into the flour, add the other dry ingredients and mix thoroughly. Make a well in the

centre of the dry ingredients, pour in the buttermilk and bicarbonate of soda and then pour the egg into the buttermilk. Blend the dry ingredients with the egg and milk, and knead the mixture to a soft dough.

Turn out on to a well floured board, knead to a large ball and flatten with the palm of the hand to form a round, flat cake, approximately half an inch thick.

Bake evenly on both sides on a moderately hot bakestone. Split in half when warm and spread thickly with butter.
Bala, Merioneth.

This cake would be prepared in Merioneth when bread was in short supply, or when friends were expected to tea.

Baking cacen gri *on the bakestone. Kennixton, Welsh Folk Museum.*

Teisen Lechwan—Bakestone Cake

one pound self-raising flour
quarter pound butter
quarter pound lard
one cupful sugar
one cupful currants
two eggs, well beaten
a little salt
a little milk

Rub the butter and lard into the flour and add all the
other dry ingredients. Mix with the beaten eggs and a
little milk to make a soft dough. Turn out on to a floured
board, roll out, and cut into small rounds. Grease the
bakestone lightly and heat moderately. (Sprinkle a little
flour on it and if it browns fairly quickly, it has reached
the correct temperature.) Bake the cakes on it, allowing
two or three minutes for each side.
Dowlais, Glamorgan.

Teisen ar y Maen—Bakestone Turnover

Prepare dough as for *teisen lechwan,* but a little less fat
and sugar may be used. Roll out to the size of a large
dinner plate. Cover one half of this with fruit (sliced
apple, blackberries or gooseberries, as available) and
fold the other half over the fruit. Press the edges of both
halves together and seal.
Bake the pie on a moderately hot bakestone until golden
brown on both sides. Split open, remove top layer of
pastry, add sugar to the fruit whilst hot and re-cover with
the baked pastry.

This cake was prepared specially on the farms during
harvest time.
Creunant, Glamorgan.

Teisen ar y Maen—Bakestone Pie

one pound flour
six ounces lard
a little salt
a little water
fruit, according to season
sugar
butter

Rub the lard into the flour, add salt and mix well with
a little water to make short pastry. Divide the pastry
into two equal parts and roll out into rounds of the
size of a dinner plate.
Clean and prepare the fruit and place evenly over one
pastry round. Cover with the second round, press the
edges of both together and seal.
Bake the pie on a moderately hot bakestone until golden
brown on both sides. Then place on a large plate or
wooden platter, and whilst hot, remove the top layer of
pastry, melt two or three tablespoonfuls of sugar and a
little butter into the fruit and re-cover with the pastry.
Serve hot or cold.
Kenfig Hill, Glamorgan.

This pie is baked in the form of a turn-over in some areas.
See *Teisen lechwan.*

Teisen ar y maen is similar to *teisen blât* (lit. plate cake),
the one being baked on the bakestone and the other
baked on a plate in the oven.

*Turning a fruit turn-over with a wooden slice. Mrs. Violet James,
Hebron, Carmarthenshire (originally of Pen-tyrch, Glamorgan).*

Leicecs—Lightcakes

four ounces flour
three ounces sugar
a little salt
one egg and a little milk or buttermilk
with quarter teaspoonful bicarbonate of soda

Put the dry ingredients in a small bowl. Beat the egg well
and add a little milk, or dissolve the bicarbonate of soda
in the buttermilk.
Make a well in the centre of the dry ingredients, pour in
the egg and milk or the buttermilk, and beat the mixture
with a fork into a thick, creamy batter.
Drop the batter from a dessertspoon, or from a jug, on to
a hot, well-greased bakestone or griddle, forming small
cakes approximately three to four inches in diameter.
Allow to bake until small bubbles appear on the surface
and the lower surface is golden brown. Then turn with a
knife and bake on the other side.
Serve warm with butter.
Bala, Merioneth.

Leicecs were an essential part of the welcome given to
visitors for afternoon tea in the counties of Denbigh,
Merioneth and Montgomery. The hostess would bake
them during the course of the afternoon and served
them warm with cups of tea.

Dropping the batter on the bakestone.

Ffroes—Pancakes

one pound plain flour
a little salt
a little nutmeg
three ounces sugar
four ounces butter
three eggs
a little warm milk
two teaspoonfuls baking powder

Mix the flour, salt, nutmeg and sugar together in a warm
basin and then rub in the butter into this dry mixture.
Add a little warm milk to the beaten eggs and gradually
pour into the dry ingredients, beating well with a wooden
spoon to make a smooth batter. If the batter appears to
be too stiff, a little warm milk may be added. Allow to

Baking lightcakes. Kennixton, Welsh Folk Museum.

stand for half an hour, and then fold in the baking powder but do not beat. Now drop gently from a tablespoon on to a moderately hot, well greased bakestone and bake the pancakes until light brown on both sides. Put on a plate, spread each with butter and sprinkle with sugar. Continue to bake the remainder of the batter in the same way.
Abercynon, Glamorgan.

Pancakes were baked generally throughout the whole of Wales but their names, in Welsh, differed widely from county to county or from district to district, namely:

cramwythen	pl. cramoth	(parts of Carmarthenshire and Glamorgan)
crempog	pl. crempogau	(in the counties of north Wales, generally)
ffroesen	pl. ffroes	(parts of Glamorgan)
poncagen	pl. poncagau	(parts of Cardiganshire)
pancogen	pl. pancocs	(parts of Pembrokeshire)
pancosen	pl. pancos	(parts of Carmarthenshire and Cardiganshire)

Ffroes—Pancakes

one pound plain flour
one ounce butter
one ounce lard
four eggs
a little milk
(currants, if desired)

Sift the flour into a bowl. Melt the butter and lard and pour into a well in the centre of the flour. Beat the eggs, add a little milk and gradually pour into the flour, beating well to make a thick, creamy batter. Then add a little water and beat again for a few seconds to make it light in consistency.
Melt an ounce of fat on a frying-pan or on a bakestone and pour on it half a cupful of batter. (A few currants may be added at this stage, if desired.) Allow the pancake to bake until small bubbles appear on its surface, then turn and bake on the other side.
Place on a plate and spread with butter and a little sugar.

Continue to bake the remainder of the batter, and pile the pancakes on the plate to keep warm.

Ffroes eira Take a cupful of clean snow instead of the water in the above recipe and fold it into the batter. The snow helps to give a light consistency.
Dowlais, Glamorgan.

It was a general tradition to prepare pancakes for afternoon tea when celebrating the birthday of any member of the family in Dowlais, as in many other districts in south Wales.

Crempog—Pancakes

ten ounces plain flour
half a teaspoonful salt
two ounces butter
three quarters of a pint of warm buttermilk
two eggs, well beaten
three ounces sugar
one teaspoonful bicarbonate of soda
one tablespoonful vinegar

Melt the butter in the warm buttermilk, pour gradually into the flour and beat well. Allow this mixture to stand for a few hours, if possible.
When ready to bake the pancakes, stir the sugar, the bicarbonate of soda and the vinegar into the beaten eggs. Pour this second mixture into the first one and beat well to make a smooth batter.
Drop the batter from a tablespoon on to a well greased and hot bakestone or griddle. Bake over a moderate heat until the pancakes are golden brown on both sides.
Then spread butter on each pancake whilst hot and serve warm. (A cupful of sour cream stirred into the batter acts as a further raising agent.)
Llanfachraeth, Anglesey.

Pancakes were an essential part of the welcome given to visitors when invited for afternoon tea in the counties of Caernarvon and Anglesey. They were also prepared there on Shrove Tuesday. On this occasion three kinds of pancakes were prepared in the farmhouses. For the master and his family *crempog wen* and *crempog furum* were served, while the servants were given *crempog surgeirch* (see respective recipes). It was also a general custom in the Lleyn peninsula on Shrove Tuesday for the children to go around from house to house singing a suitable verse at the door while begging for pancakes: e.g.

Sgwelwch chi'n dda ga i grempog?
Mae 'ngheg i'n grimpin grempog
Mae Mam rhy dlawd i brynu blawd
Mae 'Nhad rhy ddiog i weithio
'Sgwelwch chi'n dda ga i grempog?

(Please may I have some pancakes?
My mouth is parched for pancakes
My mother is too poor to buy flour
My father is too lazy to work
Please may I have some pancakes?)

Crempog Furum—Yeast Pancake

twelve ounces plain flour
two eggs
three tablespoonfuls sugar
a large knob of butter
quarter ounce yeast
a little salt
milk or buttermilk

Mix the yeast with a little sugar and warm water and leave to prove in a warm place.
Heat the milk or buttermilk and dissolve the butter in it. Sift the flour and salt into a bowl, add the sugar, make a well in the centre and pour the well-beaten eggs into it. Now gradually add the milk and beat the mixture well to make a soft, creamy batter. Lastly, add the yeast mixture and leave the batter to rise in a warm place.
Bake the pancakes on a heated bakestone or frying-pan in the usual way. Then split each pancake in half and spread with butter. Serve warm.

Crempog Surgeirch—Sour-oats Pancake

The basic ingredient used in making these sour-oats pancakes was oatmeal, or barley meal, mixed with a little plain white flour. Using a little yeast, the batter was prepared by following the same method as for *Crempog Furum* (yeast pancake) above, but was baked in the form of large thin pancakes. They were served with treacle or butter.
Capel Garmon, Denbighshire.

Slapan Sir Fôn—Anglesey Batter Cake

half a pound plain flour
two ounces sugar
two ounces currants
a pinch of salt
a pinch of bicarbonate of soda
quarter pound butter
two eggs
a little sour buttermilk

Dissolve the bicarbonate of soda in a teaspoonful of sour buttermilk. Melt the butter over a pan of hot water. Beat the eggs and pour slowly on to the melted butter and then add the sour buttermilk mixture.
Gradually pour this liquid mixture into the dry ingredients in a bowl and beat thoroughly to make a fairly stiff batter. Drop the batter from a tablespoon on to a greased bakestone or iron pan, and bake as for pancakes. Then split in half and spread with butter. Serve warm.

Slapan Dafydd—David's Batter Cake

ten ounces plain flour
two ounces butter
half a pint warm buttermilk
two eggs
three ounces sugar
three ounces sultanas
one tablespoonful vinegar
one teaspoonful bicarbonate of soda
half a teaspoonful salt

Melt the butter in the warm buttermilk. Put the flour, salt and sultanas in a bowl, gradually pour in the buttermilk mixture and beat well. Leave this mixture to stand for a few hours, if possible.
When ready to bake the cake, beat the eggs, add the sugar, soda and vinegar and then pour this second mixture into the first one, beating well.
Pour all the mixture on to a greased, moderately hot bakestone to make one large cake. Bake and turn as for pancakes. Then split in half while warm and spread with butter.
Llanfachraeth, Anglesey.

Bara Ceirch—Oatcakes

Oatcakes are common to all Celtic countries, but the art of making them varies considerably from country to country and indeed from region to region within the country. Basically, the ingredients of oatmeal and water, and sometimes a little fat, are mixed to form a dough which is finally baked on a bakestone. The art lies in the rolling out of the dough to form large, wafer-thin rounds with fine, even edges. It seems that two different methods of rolling out were adopted in Wales: the one method still practised in Merioneth today (which was also typical of the counties of north Wales) and the other practised during the first quarter of this century in certain districts of Carmarthenshire and Cardiganshire. Both methods are described in the two following recipes:

one eggcupful luke-warm water
half a teaspoonful bacon dripping
three handfuls oatmeal

Melt the dripping in the water and then gradually add the oatmeal, kneading the mixture to a soft dough. Turn out on to a wooden board sprinkled with a little oatmeal and mould the dough between the two hands to form a small cone. Flatten the cone with the palm of the hand to form a small round cake. Keeping this basic shape, proceed to roll out with a rolling pin. To ensure even rolling, give the cake an occasional quarter turn, paying particular attention to the fine edge. Roll out to a large thin oatcake, approximately ten inches in diameter.
Place the oatcake on a moderately hot griddle or bakestone and bake on both sides until it acquires a light golden colour. Finally, allow it to harden in a warm place before storing.
Bala, Merioneth.

In the counties of north Wales generally, a favourite way of eating an oatcake was to put a large piece between two slices of bread or on top of one slice of ordinary bread to make a sandwich. These sandwiches were given colloquial names such as *brechdan gaerog, brechdan linsi, brechdan fetal, piogen* and *pioden.*

The oatcake used as the basic ingredient in the dishes known as *brwes, siot* and *picws mali* is similar to the one described above but it does not contain any fat. Rolled out into a slightly thicker cake, it is more easily crushed when preparing these dishes (see respective recipes).

1

Rolling oatcakes (1-4)
Mrs. Catrin Evans, Llanuwchllyn, Merioneth.

2

Turning oatcakes with a crafell *(a wooden slice) and drying them on an oatcake rack.*

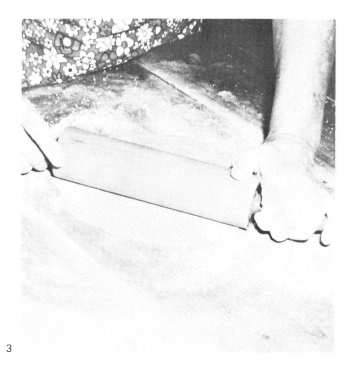

oatmeal
cold water

Put a large quantity of oatmeal in a bowl and mix gradually with cold water to form a fairly stiff dough. Knead well. Turn out on a board sprinkled with oatmeal and roll out with both hands to form a long, thick roll. Divide the roll into several equal parts and make them into small balls. Flatten each ball under the palms of the hands (as illustrated) and then place in a pile with a thick layer of oatmeal between each one. Proceed to flatten the cakes by pressing on the pile with the palm of the right hand and keeping the left hand cupped around the pile to ensure an even round shape, giving it a quarter turn at regular intervals. Finally, press down with the forearm until the cakes are about ten inches in

Rolling oatcakes (1-5)
Mrs. May Davies, Llan-saint, Carmarthenshire.

Preparing a miner's tuck-box. Teisen lap *was a regular favourite.* >

5

Put the flour and oatmeal in a large, warm bowl or jug. Melt the butter into the milk over a low heat. Cream the sugar and yeast, add the warm water and pour into the milk and melted butter. Add the beaten eggs to this liquid mixture, and pour gradually into the flour. Beat well and then allow the batter to rise in a warm place for a short period.
Grease a moderately hot bakestone, pour the batter on it as for pancakes and bake on both sides.

It was a tradition in Anglesey on Shrove Tuesday to serve *bara bwff* to the men-servants while the family enjoyed pancakes for tea.
Anglesey.

Teisen Dinca—Tinker's Cake

one pound plain flour
eight ounces butter
six ounces demerara sugar
eight ounces shredded apple
a little salt
a little milk

Rub the butter into the flour and work in the apple, sugar and salt. Mix with a little milk and knead to a fairly stiff dough.
Roll out on a floured board to make large rounds of approximately one third of an inch thick. Bake on a moderately hot bakestone for about three to four minutes on each side. Then sprinkle with sugar and cut into squares.
Gwaelod-y-garth, Glamorgan.

Alternatively, mix the above ingredients with a beaten egg and a little milk to give a softer consistency (similar to that of *teisen lap*) and bake in a hot oven. Traditionally this mixture would be baked in the Dutch oven, in front of the fire.
Pen-tyrch, Glamorgan.

diameter. Now separate the cakes carefully and brush off any loose oatmeal. Bake on a moderately hot bakestone and then dry in a warm place before storing.
Ferryside, Carmarthenshire.

Bara Bwff—Oatmeal Pancakes

eight ounces plain flour
three ounces oatmeal or wholemeal flour
three quarter ounce yeast
one teaspoonful sugar
one teaspoonful salt
two ounces butter
quarter pint milk
quarter pint warm water
two eggs, well beaten

Sgons Enwyn—Buttermilk Scones

one pound plain flour
three or four ounces butter
three ounces sugar
a little bicarbonate of soda
buttermilk

Rub the butter into the flour, and work in the other dry ingredients. Mix with buttermilk and knead to a soft dough.
Roll out on a floured board and cut into small rounds, approximately a quarter of an inch thick. Bake on a moderately hot bakestone and serve warm.
Heol Senni, Breconshire.

Teisen Ddim—Buttermilk Scone

one pound plain flour
quarter pound lard
a little salt
buttermilk

Rub the lard into the flour and salt, mix with buttermilk and knead to a soft dough.
Roll out on a floured board to make a large round of about a quarter of an inch thick, or alternatively cut into small rounds. Bake on a moderately hot bakestone. Spread with butter and serve warm.
Llandeilo'r-fân and Heol Senni, Breconshire.

Teisennau Afal—Apple Cakes

half a pound self-raising flour
quarter pound butter
quarter pound lard
five ounces sugar
one egg and a little milk
quarter teaspoonful salt
half a pound cooking apples

Rub the butter and the lard into the flour and add the salt and sugar. Peel and cut up the apples finely and work into the dry mixture. Gradually add the beaten egg and milk to make a fairly stiff dough. Roll out thinly and cut into small squares. Bake on both sides on a moderately hot bakestone and sprinkle with a little sugar.
Gower Peninsula.

Cacen Gaws—Cheese Cake

one and a half pints milk
one dessertspoonful rennet

two tablespoonfuls sugar
one egg
three ounces currants
one teaspoonful spice
short-crust pastry

Warm the milk, add the rennet and stir evenly. Allow to cool and set. Drain the curd through a muslin bag and add to it the beaten egg, sugar and currants.
Roll out pastry into rounds. Spread the mixture fairly thickly over one half of each round and fold the remainder of the pastry over it to make a small turn over. Seal the edges and bake on a fairly hot bakestone.

These cakes were baked by the Gower housewives, more especially on the farms when they had a plentiful supply of milk.
Gower Peninsula.

Bara Tato—Potato Bread

one pound potatoes
four ounces flour
two ounces sugar
one ounce butter
two ounces currants
a little milk

Boil the potatoes and mash thoroughly. Melt the butter into the potatoes and fold in the other dry ingredients. Add a little milk, if necessary, to make a soft dough. Turn out on to a well-floured board and roll out into large, fairly thin rounds. Bake on a fairly hot bakestone until golden brown on both sides. Spread with butter.
Dinas Cross, Pembrokeshire.

It was common practice in many districts in Pembrokeshire and Cardiganshire to make this cake when there was a considerable amount of potatoes left over after the mid-day meal.

Pice'r Pregethwr—Drop Scones

four ounces self-raising flour
three ounces butter
two eggs
half a pint buttermilk or milk

Rub the butter into the flour, gradually add the beaten eggs and milk, beating well to make a smooth batter. Allow to stand overnight.

Drop the batter from a tablespoon on to a hot bakestone and bake as for pancakes.

Serve warm, spread thickly with butter.

Holyhead, Anglesey.

Teisen Hufen—Cream Cake

four ounces flour
one and a half ounces sugar
one egg
fresh cream

Put the dry ingredients in a large basin, break the egg into a well in the centre and beat with a fork. Fold in the fresh cream to make a light batter.

Grease a moderately hot bakestone and drop the batter on to it from a large spoon. Bake on both sides until golden brown.

These cakes were prepared by the farmers' wives in north Glamorgan as a treat on special occasions only.

Rhigos, Glamorgan.

In the Vale of Glamorgan this same batter was baked in the Dutch oven in front of the fire. Today it may be baked in a shallow tin placed in a low position under a fairly hot grill.

Cakes

Teisen Dorth—Loaf Cake

pound and a half plain flour
half a pound butter
quarter pound lard
one and a half cupfuls brown sugar
half a pound raisins
half a pound sultanas
half a pound currants
a little nutmeg and cinnamon
a little grated lemon peel
six eggs, well beaten
one and a half ounces yeast
a little salt

Cream the yeast with a teaspoonful of sugar in a small basin. Mix with a little warm water, cover and put in a warm place to prove.
Wash and dry the fruit, and quarter the raisins, if large. Rub the butter and lard into the flour, add the fruit and other dry ingredients and work through the flour. Make a well in the centre of this dry mixture and pour in the yeast. Add the well-beaten eggs and work all together to make a moist dough. A little warm milk and water may be added if necessary. Cover the dough and leave to rise in a warm place. Then divide it into equal parts and put in warm greased tins.
Leave to rise in the tins for a further hour, and then bake in a moderately hot oven for an hour, or longer according to the size of the loaves.
Dowlais, Glamorgan.

Loaf cake was synonymous with Christmas celebrations in the industrial valleys of south Wales. The dough, prepared in large quantities, would be carried to the local bakehouse where the baker would be responsible for baking the cakes for a penny or two per loaf.
Neighbours were invited to taste each other's cake, and tradition has it (in the district of Margam, near Port Talbot) that if a young maid was given the opportunity to taste thirteen different cakes in one season she would marry before the following Christmas.

Teisen Dorth—Loaf Cake

a large piece of freshly risen dough
lard or butter
brown sugar
currants
raisins
a little spice
one egg, well beaten

Having kept a large piece of freshly risen dough, work in the butter or lard and then the other dry ingredients. Add the beaten egg, knead and leave to rise in a warm place. Put in a warm, greased tin and bake in a moderately hot oven, as for bread.
A simple method of making loaf cake, commonly practised in farmhouses at harvest time.
Margam, Glamorgan.

Torth Fraith—Fruit Cake

one pound flour
a little salt
a little brown sugar
half a pound currants
half a pound raisins
one tablespoonful black treacle
one ounce yeast
warm water
(a little butter or lard, optional)

Cream the yeast with a little sugar, mix with a little tepid water and set aside for a few minutes until it becomes frothy.
Melt the treacle (and fat) in a little warm water. Put all the dry ingredients in a bowl and work the sugar, salt and fruit through the flour. Make a well in the centre, pour in the yeast and mix to a soft dough, adding the treacled water as necessary. Knead well, cover and leave to rise in a warm place for about an hour or longer. Turn out on to a floured board, knead well and then put into a greased, warm tin. Leave to rise for a further thirty minutes and then put into a fairly hot oven. Bake as for bread.

When cold, slice and spread with butter.
Uwchmynydd, Caernarvonshire.

Teisen Lap—Lap Cake

one pound plain flour
half a pound lard (or a quarter pound each of lard and butter)
one large cupful brown sugar
one cupful currants
a little salt
a little nutmeg
two eggs, well beaten
buttermilk

Rub the fat into the flour, and work in all the other dry ingredients. Make a well in the centre, and pour in the eggs. Gradually add the buttermilk to the mixture and beat with a wooden spoon. The consistency should be sufficiently soft and moist for the batter to drop easily from the spoon. Put the mixture into a greased shallow tin and bake in a moderately hot oven.
Pen-prysg, Glamorgan.

This cake was traditionally baked in a Dutch oven before an open fire in the district of Pen-prysg, Pencoed. The mixture was poured into the shallow tin at the bottom of the oven and then baked slowly on a stand in front of the fire. A similar method could be adopted today by putting the mixture in a shallow tin and baking it under a hot grill.

Teisen lap was regarded as an 'ordinary' cake baked fairly regularly in the coal-mining villages of south Wales. It stood the miner in good stead as a 'sweet' for his mid-day meal underground and the moist texture of the cake prevented it from crumbling in his tuck-box. The name *teisen lap* describes the texture of the cake as the adjective *llap*, now almost extinct, means *moist* or *wet.*

Teisen Lap—Lap Cake

one pound plain flour
a little baking powder
a little salt
half a pound butter and a little lard
three quarter pound currants
a large cupful sugar
four eggs
a little milk

Rub the fat in the flour and work in the other dry ingredients. Separate the yolks from the egg whites and beat separately, pour together and beat again. Make a well in the centre of the dry ingredients, pour in the beaten eggs and gradually add a little milk to make a fairly soft, moist mixture. (The consistency should be sufficiently moist for the mixture to drop easily from the spoon.) Grease a shallow tin, pour in the mixture and bake in a hot oven. (The cake will be light if baked fairly sharply.)
Dowlais, Glamorgan.

This cake was baked on an *enamel plate* in many districts, as for example in Ystalyfera, Glamorgan.

Teisen Lap—Lap Cake

one pint sour cream
four tablespoonfuls self-raising flour
four ounces sugar
three ounces butter
four ounces sultanas
one egg, well beaten

Rub the fat into the flour and work into the sour cream, together with the other dry ingredients. Lastly, add the beaten egg to the mixture before pouring it into a shallow tin. Bake in a slow oven or in a low position under a hot grill. Traditionally this mixture was baked slowly in a Dutch oven in front of an open fire.
Kenfig Hill, Glamorgan.

This cake was known as *teisen hufen* (cream cake) in some districts in Glamorgan.

Cacen Waed Gwyddau—Goose Blood Tart

short-crust pastry
blood from a number of geese
one pound currants
one pound soft brown sugar
half a pound shredded suet
three teaspoonfuls mixed spice
four wooden spoonfuls golden syrup
a little salt

Keep the blood of about three geese in a greased basin and immerse this basin in a saucepan half full of water. Boil for about three hours and then allow the blood to cool and set in the basin.
Take approximately half a pound of the solidified blood and rub it between the fingers to make fine crumbs.
Then add to it the syrup and all other ingredients and mix well with a wooden spoon.
Spread this mixture thickly between two layers of pastry on a plate or shallow tin and bake in a hot oven for approximately half an hour.
Trefeglwys, Montgomeryshire.

Oral evidence testifies that this cake was an essential part of the Christmas fare in the Trefeglwys district and

similarly in the districts of Staylittle, Llanbryn Mair and Llangurig in Montgomeryshire. To date, however, there is no evidence to show that it was prepared in any other county in Wales.

Tarten Bwmpen—Marrow Pie

a marrow
sugar
currants
short-crust pastry

Peel, clean and slice the marrow and boil in a little water until soft. Drain well and leave to cool before mashing it with a fork.
Line an oven-proof plate with pastry and cover with the prepared marrow. (Do not be too generous as the marrow mixture is watery and tends to 'run' when cooking.) Add a thick layer of sugar and dot with a few currants. Cover with a second layer of pastry, press edges of pastry layers together and seal. Bake in a hot oven.
Bardsey Island.

Cacen Gneifio—Shearing Cake

half a pound plain flour
six ounces moist sugar
four ounces butter
peel of half a lemon, grated
one egg, well beaten
quarter pint milk
one teaspoonful baking powder
two teaspoonfuls caraway seeds
a little nutmeg

Rub the fat into the flour, add the other dry ingredients and mix with the beaten egg and milk. Line a cake tin with greaseproof paper and put the mixture into it. Bake in a moderately hot oven for approximately one hour.
Lampeter, Cardiganshire.

Cacen Gneifio neu Ddyrnu— Shearing or Threshing Cake

three large cupfuls plain flour
half a pound sugar
half a pound bacon dripping
a little bicarbonate of soda, dissolved in a little tepid
water and buttermilk
one pound dried fruit (currants and raisins)
two or three eggs, well beaten
buttermilk

Rub the fat into the flour and work in the other dry ingredients. Mix gradually with the beaten eggs and add sufficient buttermilk to give a fairly soft consistency. Grease a cake tin, put the mixture into it and bake in a fairly hot oven for approximately an hour and a half.
Llanerfyl, Montgomeryshire.

Cacen Llaeth Berw—Boiled Milk Cake

one pound flour
half a pound butter
six ounces brown sugar
half a pound currants
half a pound raisins
a little spice
three eggs
half a pint boiling milk
half a teaspoonful bicarbonate of soda

Rub the fat into the flour and work in the other dry ingredients. Beat the eggs and pour into the dry mixture. Gradually add the boiling milk (with the soda dissolved in it) and beat the mixture well. Put into a greased cake tin and bake in a hot oven.
Whitchurch, Glamorgan.

Cacen Llaeth Enwyn—Buttermilk Cake

one pound flour
half a pound butter
half a pound currants
half a pound sultanas

two ounces candied peel
half a pound brown sugar
half a pint buttermilk
a little baking powder or bicarbonate of soda
a little spice, optional

Rub the butter into the flour and work in all the other dry ingredients. Gradually add the buttermilk to give a fairly stiff mixture.
Line a cake tin with greaseproof paper, put the mixture into it and bake in a moderately hot oven for an hour and a half or two hours.

It was possible to prepare this cake when eggs were in short supply.
Cellan, Cardiganshire.

Cacen Lard—Lardy Cake

one pound freshly made dough
eight ounces lard
four ounces currants
two ounces candied peel
two ounces sugar

Put the dough on a well-floured board and roll out into an oblong shape to a thickness of about one inch. Divide the other ingredients into four equal parts and work into the dough in the following way: spread two ounces of lard evenly on the dough and cover with an ounce of currants and half an ounce of peel. Sprinkle with half an ounce of sugar and a little flour and then fold the dough in two, covering the fat, fruit, etc. Roll out again to its original oblong shape, spread on it the proportion of lard, fruit etc and fold. Repeat this process twice again, handling the dough as lightly as possible. Then put the dough on a shallow tin or tray and bake in a fairly hot oven for approximately one hour. Cut into small squares, spread with butter and serve hot or cold, as desired.
Ton Pentre, Glamorgan.

A popular cake, made regularly on bread-baking day in parts of Glamorgan.

Cacen Gyrens—Currant Cake

short-crust pastry
currants
sugar
black treacle

Line an oven-proof plate with pastry, rolled out fairly thinly. Cover with a thick layer of currants and add sugar and black treacle to taste. Seal with a second layer of pastry and bake in a hot oven.

Cacen gyrens would be one of the cakes prepared for Sunday tea on Bardsey Island.
Bardsey Island.

Cacen Goch—Treacle Cake

half a pound plain flour
two and a half ounces butter
four ounces mixed fruit
one tablespoonful black treacle
two tablespoonfuls sugar
a little mixed spice
milk or buttermilk

Rub the butter into the flour, work in the other dry ingredients and gradually add the milk (or buttermilk) together with the treacle to give a fairly stiff mixture. Put the mixture on a greased *enamel* (or oven-proof) plate and bake in a moderately hot oven for approximately one hour.

Another name given to this particular cake on Bardsey Island was *tamad* (lit. piece), and it was eaten quite regularly for afternoon tea there.
Bardsey Island.

Teisen Ffwrdd â Hi—A Quick-mix Cake

two ounces butter
two ounces sugar
two ounces currants
half a pound plain flour
a pinch of salt
milk

Rub the fat into the flour and add the other dry ingredients. Mix gradually with a little milk to give a fairly soft consistency.
Put the mixture into a greased, shallow tin and bake in a moderately hot oven.

Alternatively, keep the mixture fairly stiff and spread evenly on a moderately hot bakestone. Bake on both sides and then split open while warm and spread with butter.
Anglesey.

Teisen Te Deg—Elevenses Cake

half a pound plain flour
three ounces sugar
two ounces butter
two ounces lard
one egg
half a cupful milk
half a teaspoonful salt
half a teaspoonful bicarbonate of soda

Cream the fat and sugar, add the egg and beat together. Gradually add the flour, salt and soda and mix with a little milk to give a fairly soft consistency. (Some two ounces of currants may be added, if desired.) Put the mixture in a greased cake tin and bake in a moderately hot oven for approximately one hour.

A cake specially prepared for the mid-morning break in the Lampeter district.
Lampeter, Cardiganshire.

Poten Dato—Potato Cake

potatoes, boiled in salt water
milk
one egg, well beaten
sugar
currants
plain flour
spice
water
a little salt

Loaf cake, the rich, yeast fruit cake baked for Christmas in the counties of south Wales. >

Drain the potatoes and put in a large bowl. Add a few lumps of butter and mash thoroughly. Proceed to add the other dry ingredients (quantities vary according to personal taste) and mix with the beaten egg and a little milk to give a fairly soft consistency.

Put the mixture into a greased shallow tin and bake in a moderately hot oven.

Newport, Pembrokeshire.

Poten dato was baked regularly in the counties of Cardiganshire and Pembrokeshire where potatoes were plentiful in the autumn. Prepared in large quantities it would be baked in the brick wall-oven. This oven would be heated at least once a week for baking bread and as the bricks retained some heat for several hours it was generally the custom to bake cakes and puddings in this 'after heat' overnight.

Miogod Sir Benfro—Pembrokeshire Buns

one pound flour
one ounce yeast
two ounces sugar
half an ounce lard
half an ounce butter
two ounces currants
one ounce candied peel
warm milk and water mixture

Rub the fat into the flour and add the other dry ingredients. Dissolve the yeast in a little warm water and pour into a well in the centre of the dry mixture. Add the milk and water mixture gradually and work with the yeast into the dry ingredients to make a soft dough.
Leave to rise in a warm place for about fifteen minutes. Then knead on a floured board, and divide to form small balls. Roll them out lightly with a rolling pin and allow to rise again for a further ten minutes.
Bake in a hot oven for about twenty minutes until golden brown.
Rhiwbina, Glamorgan.

These small buns, known also as *cace* were given to children as part of their *calennig* (New Year's gift) on New Year's Day in many districts in Pembrokeshire.

The housewife would bake them in large quantities for this special occasion and the children would carry them home in clean pillow cases on their backs. Generally, each child would be given some two cakes at every house after he had wished the members of the household a very happy New Year. These wishes were frequently conveyed in verse or song.

Teisen Griwsion—Cree Cake

one pound self-raising flour
three quarter pound finely diced cree
half a pound sugar
a little milk and water

Put all the dry ingredients in a mixing bowl and gradually add the milk and water mixture to make a soft dough.
Turn out on to a well-floured board and roll out to a thickness of about one inch.
Place in a greased shallow tin, sprinkle with a little sugar and then bake in a moderately hot oven for about half an hour.
Swansea, Glamorgan.

Adding a small quantity of currants to the above recipe, and baking the rolled out dough on the bakestone was a common practice in other districts.
Gower Peninsula.

Lard procured from the layers of fat around the pig's abdomen was invaluable to the housewife for making cakes and pastry. These layers, cut into small pieces and placed in a large saucepan or boiler, were melted down gradually over a low heat. The fat was then poured through a fine sieve and stored in earthenware jars or in any other suitable container. The pig's bladder would be used for this purpose in many districts.
The small, crisp pieces left over when all the lard was rendered were commonly known in Welsh as *criwson* or *creision*. *Cree, scruggins* and *scrutchins* were the English equivalents used in different parts of Wales. Tossed in oatmeal and seasoned with salt and pepper, they were eaten with bread and butter. Alternatively they were put in a cake mixture instead of ordinary fat.

Dinca Fala—Apple Cake

ten ounces self-raising flour
five ounces butter
five ounces demerara sugar
one pound cooking apples, finely diced
a little milk

Rub the butter into the flour and add the sugar and the diced apple. Mix with a little milk to make a fairly stiff dough. Grease a shallow tin, flatten the dough evenly into it and bake in a moderately hot oven for approximately half an hour.
Whitchurch, Glamorgan.

Traditionally this cake would be baked in a Dutch oven in front of an open fire in some districts in Glamorgan.

Teisen Reis—Rice Cake

two cupfuls rice
a little salt
water
one pound plain flour
half a pound butter
one teaspoonful baking powder
four eggs
milk
sugar—according to taste
a little nutmeg

Boil the rice in salted water until soft and fluffy. Rub the fat into the flour and then work in the rice and the other dry ingredients. Finally add the eggs and a little milk to give a light batter consistency. Then pour the batter into a greased shallow tin and bake in a fairly hot oven. Alternatively place in a low position under a hot grill. Traditionally this cake was baked in a Dutch oven in front of an open fire.
Nantgarw, Glamorgan.

Teisen Mêl a Sinsir—
Honey and Ginger Cake

four cupfuls plain flour
two large teaspoonfuls baking powder
two large teaspoonfuls ground ginger

half a cupful sultanas
half a cupful cherries (halved)
a little candied peel
four ounces butter
two eggs
three-quarter cupful honey
a little salt
a little milk

Sift the flour, the baking powder, salt and ginger into a bowl and add the dried fruit, candied peel and cherries. Melt the butter over a low heat and dissolve the honey into it with a little milk. Leave to cool and then pour, together with the beaten eggs, into the dry mixture. Mix thoroughly.
Put in a greased cake tin and bake in a moderately hot oven. Store for a fortnight before cutting.
Llanwenog, Cardiganshire.

Teisennau 'Berffro—'Berffro Cakes

two ounces caster sugar
four ounces butter
six ounces flour

Soften the butter and work in the sugar by hand. Add the flour, a little at a time, again mixing by hand, the warmth of the hand keeping the mixture soft and pliable. Then put on a lightly-floured board, and divide equally into small balls.
Take a scallop shell, sprinkle with a little sugar and press each ball against its base to make a thin, fan-shaped cake. Place the cakes on a greased, shallow tin, with a generous space between each one. Bake in a hot oven for a few minutes only—they should not turn brown. Sprinkle with caster sugar while warm.
Bryngwran, Anglesey.

Cacen Ann Dafis—Ann Davies' Cake

one pound and a half plain flour
one pound and a half currants
one pound sugar
quarter pound butter
half a pound lard
half a teaspoonful nutmeg
half a teaspoonful mixed spice

half a teaspoonful baking powder
quarter teaspoonful salt
half a pint milk
two eggs, well beaten

Rub the butter and lard into the flour and sugar and add all the other dry ingredients. Make a well in the centre of this mixture, pour the eggs into it and gradually add the milk, mixing all together to give a fairly soft consistency.
Grease two cake tins, divide the mixture equally between them and bake in a moderately hot oven for about one and a half hours.

Ann Davies kept a shop in Kidwelly at the beginning of this century. She baked bread and cakes in a large oven behind the shop and her fruit cake (recipe as above) was in great demand, at sixpence per pound.
Miss Davies died in the Spring of 1928.
Kidwelly, Carmarthenshire.

Teisen Dros Nos—Overnight Cake

half a pound plain flour
four ounces butter or lard
three or four ounces mixed dried fruit
one teaspoonful cinnamon
one teaspoonful ginger
half a teaspoonful bicarbonate of soda
one tablespoonful vinegar
milk

Rub the fat into the flour and work in the other dry ingredients. Mix gradually with milk to give a fairly soft consistency. Dissolve the soda in the vinegar, pour it over the soft batter mixture and stir briskly. Allow this mixture to stand overnight.
Line a cake tin with greaseproof paper, pour the mixture into it and bake in a moderately hot oven for about one and a quarter hours.
Caernarvon.

Bread

Bara Gwyn—White Bread

three and a half pounds plain flour
three teaspoonfuls salt
four teaspoonfuls sugar
one and a half pints warm water
one ounce yeast

Put the flour and salt in a warm bowl. Cream the yeast
and sugar and pour into a well in the centre of the flour.
Cover the yeast mixture with a little of the flour, and
leave in a warm place until it becomes frothy. Then
proceed to mix the dough, adding the warm water
gradually. Knead well for about ten minutes until the
hands and sides of the bowl are free of dough. Cover the
bowl and leave in a warm place until the dough has
doubled its original size. Then turn it out on to a floured
board, divide and mould into loaves according to the
size of the tins. Put each loaf into a warm, greased tin
and leave to rise again for another half hour. Then bake
the loaves in a moderately hot oven for approximately
one and a half hours, according to size.
Breconshire.

On bread baking day, some housewives would keep a
little dough and bake a small batch on the bakestone or
griddle. This batch loaf would be eaten fresh for tea on
that day. It was known as *bara planc* (Cwm Gwaun),
bara mân (Bryn, Port Talbot), *picen ar y lychwan*
(Tonyrefail), adopting the Welsh name used for the
bakestone in specific areas. *Bara prwmlid* was the name
given to it in Pen-prysg, near Pen-coed.
Similarly, small batches would be baked on the floor of
the oven. Their sizes varied and the Welsh name by

which these loaves were known again differed, e.g. *bara
bricen* (Pren-gwyn), *cwgen* (Brynberian), *torth gwaelod
popty* (Rhydymain), *torth ar fflat y ffwrn* (Ystalyfera),
torth ar llawr y ffwrn (Kenfig Hill), *sôts* (Dowlais) and
hogen (Bwlch-llan).

Mixing the dough. Miss Margied Jones, Llanuwchllyn, Merioneth.

2

Baking the bread in a wall oven.

3

Loaves drying out before storing.

Another common baking day custom was to keep a small quantity of the dough and use it as a base for a currant loaf cake. The usual method of preparing it was to work a little lard, sugar and currants (according to taste) into the dough and knead it well. It was then covered with a clean cloth and left to rise in a warm place (as for bread). Finally it was shaped into a large loaf and baked in a tin in a moderately hot oven. Alternatively it was divided into small batches or buns which were baked on the floor of the oven or on a hot bakestone. This particular cake or currant bread was known by different names, e.g. *teisen fara* (Tonyrefail), *torth fach* (Rhoslan), *teisen dôs cwnnad* (Bryn, by Port Talbot), *cacen does* (Llanbedr, by Harlech), *teisen does* (Bryncroes), *torth gyrens* (Llanuwchllyn), *torth gri* (Mynytho), *bara cwrens* (Brynberian), *cwgen gyrens* (New Quay), *pics* (Cross Inn), *picen* (Gelli-wen) and *pice cyrens* (Ystalyfera).

Bara Planc—Griddle Bread

two pounds plain flour
quarter teaspoonful salt
quarter teaspoonful sugar
one ounce dried yeast
a little warm milk
a little warm water

Sift the flour, sugar and salt into a warm bowl. Soften the yeast in a little warm water and put aside for a few minutes until it becomes frothy. Then pour the yeasted water into the flour and mix the dough gradually, adding warm milk as needed and kneading well until soft in texture. Cover and leave to rise in a warm place for approximately one and a half hours.
Divide the dough and shape into round, flat loaves—do not make them too thick. Bake on both sides on a moderately hot bakestone.
Crymych, Pembrokeshire.

Bara Can—White Bread

one pound white flour
half an ounce dried yeast
a little warm water
one ounce butter
one egg, well beaten
a little salt
half a pint warm milk

Baking bread on a bakestone. Mrs. Rachel Thomas, Manordeilo, Carmarthenshire.

Rub the butter into the flour and add the salt. Blend the yeast in warm water and pour into a well in the centre of the flour. Add the beaten egg and the warm milk to the yeasted water and beat again with a wooden spoon. Now gradually work in the flour to make a soft dough. Knead well and shape into one large loaf. Put it in a greased tin and leave in a warm place until the dough has risen to twice its original size. Bake the loaf in a hot oven for approximately one hour.
Rhydlewis, Cardiganshire.

This loaf was prepared as a luxury for Sunday tea.
Llanrhystud, Cardiganshire.

Bara Gwenith—Wheat Bread

two pounds wholemeal flour
three quarter ounce dried yeast
a little sugar
pinch of salt
a knob of butter (optional)
one pint warm water

Put the flour and salt in a warm bowl and rub the butter into it, if used. Cream the sugar and yeast until moist and blend with a little warm water. Pour the yeast mixture into a well in the centre of the dry ingredients, cover it with a little flour and leave to stand in a warm place for twenty to thirty minutes. Then knead into a soft dough, using the remainder of the water as required. Return the bowl to a warm place and allow the dough to rise for an hour. Then turn it out on to a floured board and knead quickly for two minutes. Divide the dough into two equal parts, place in greased, warmed tins and allow to rise for another half hour. Then bake the loaves in a hot oven for approximately one hour, according to size.
Bala, Merioneth.

Bara Cymysg—Maslin Bread

three pounds white flour
one pound barley meal
one ounce dried yeast
salt dissolved in warm water

Crumble the yeast into a little warm water to soften it. Mix together the two kinds of flour in a large bowl, make a well in the centre and pour in the yeasted water. Sprinkle a little flour over it, cover the bowl with a clean cloth and leave to stand for about twenty minutes until the yeast becomes frothy. Then, gradually add the warm, salted water to make a soft dough. Knead thoroughly, for a longer period than is usual for ordinary dough. Cover and allow to rise for approximately one hour. Divide the dough and shape into loaves according to the size of the tins. Put the loaves in greased tins and bake them in a hot oven.
Llanfachraeth, Anglesey.

In Anglesey, these loaves were traditionally baked singly on a bakestone, but were covered with an inverted cast-iron pan. Using gorse or straw as fuel, the fire was lit in a sheltered position outside the house or on the hearth in the kitchen. The bakestone would rest on a tripod stand over the fire and the inverted pan would be covered with glowing embers so that the loaf would be completely enclosed in heat. *Pobi yn y baw* (baking in dirt) was the local idiom used to describe this particular method of baking in this part of Wales. Barley bread was baked in the same way on the Llŷn peninsula, but the fuel varied according to what was available, e.g. chaff, gorse or charred furze. The loaves were named *torth padell a gradell* (griddle and pan loaf) or *torth dan badell* (loaf under a pan). In other areas where peat was the main source of fuel, bread was similarly baked in a pot oven, glowing embers being placed on the lid of the pot as well as beneath it. In this instance the loaf would adopt the Welsh name given to the pot in respective areas, e.g. *torth ffwrn fach, torth getel, torth grochan* or it would refer to the fuel used for baking it—e.g. *bara twarch a mate* (Pembrokeshire).

Bara Crai—Unleavened Bread

one pound plain, white flour
half a teaspoonful salt
half a teaspoonful bicarbonate of soda
half a pint buttermilk
(a few currants, optional)

Put the flour in a bowl and work in the salt and currants. Dissolve the soda in the warm buttermilk and pour it gradually into the flour. Mix all together to make a soft dough. Knead it lightly and turn it out on to a floured board. Shape the dough into a round flat loaf, rolling it lightly with a rolling pin. Put the loaf on a greased, hot bakestone or heavy frying pan and bake until the surface begins to harden. Turn and bake on the other side.
Upper Banwy, Montgomeryshire.

This unleavened bread was commonly prepared as a stop gap when the week's supply of bread fell short before the regular baking day. The ingredients varied slightly, according to local custom—water was used as an alternative to buttermilk for mixing it, and sugar and currants were optional extras in some areas. The name by which it was known was closely linked with these ingredients, e.g. *bara llaeth enwyn* (buttermilk bread—Crug-y-bar), *bara soda* (soda bread—Pennant, Llanbryn Mair), *bara trw'r dŵr* (bread through water—Abergorlech), or it was known simply as *bara crai* (Aberaeron), or *bara cri* (unleavened bread—Bont Dolgadfan).

Bara Surgeirch—Sour Oatmeal Bread

half a bowlful wholemeal flour
half a teaspoonful bicarbonate of soda

a little sugar and salt
a little oatmeal
a little buttermilk

Put all the dry ingredients, except the oatmeal, in a large bowl and mix thoroughly. Sift the oatmeal into the bowl over the other ingredients and gradually add the buttermilk, mixing all together to make a fairly soft batter. (It should drop off the spoon fairly easily.) Pour it into a greased, hot frying pan and bake the loaf on both sides over a moderate heat.
Dyffryn Ardudwy, Merioneth.

Bara Brith—Currant Bread

three pounds plain, white flour
two ounces dried yeast
fourteen ounces brown sugar
eight ounces lard
two ounces butter
one pound each of currants, sultanas and raisins
three ounces candied peel
one dessertspoonful black treacle
three teaspoonfuls salt
two eggs, well beaten
warm water

Mix the yeast and treacle in a little warm water and allow to 'prove' in a warm place. Melt the lard and butter, and add the beaten eggs and sugar to them. Put the flour, dried fruit and salt in a warm bowl, and add the prepared liquid mixtures gradually, mixing all together thoroughly to make a soft dough. Knead well, cover and allow to rise in a warm place for some three hours.
Then turn out on to a floured board, divide and shape into loaves according to the size of the tins. Put the dough into warm and greased tins and allow to rise again in these tins until it becomes twice its original size. Bake the loaves in a very hot oven (450°F) for the first hour, reduce heat to 400°F for the second hour and to 300°F for the third hour.
Llanfachraeth, Anglesey.

Bara Brith—Currant Bread

one pound plain flour
three ounces butter

three ounces sugar
a little salt
six ounces mixed fruit
half an ounce dried yeast
half a pint milk
one egg, well beaten
a little nutmeg

Melt the butter in the milk over a low heat. Put all the dry ingredients in a warm bowl together with the yeast, rubbed into fine crumbs. Add the egg to the warm milk and butter and pour this mixture gradually into the dry ingredients, to make a soft dough. Cover and allow to rise in a warm place until it is twice its original size. Then knead the dough lightly on a floured board and shape into loaves according to the size of the tins. Put into greased tins and allow to rise again for a short period. Bake in a moderately hot oven for approximately one hour, according to the size of each loaf.
Cardigan.

Bara Brith—Currant Bread

two pounds plain flour
one ounce yeast
twelve ounces butter
six ounces soft brown sugar
six ounces currants
six ounces sultanas
three ounces raisins
two ounces candied peel
quarter teaspoonful nutmeg or mixed spice
half a teaspoonful salt
two eggs
one dessertspoonful black treacle
a little warm milk and warm water

Put the flour in a mixing bowl and allow to stand in a warm place for a short while. Rub the butter into the flour, add all the other dry ingredients and mix thoroughly. Cream the yeast with a little sugar in a smaller basin and blend it with half a cupful of warm milk. Make a well in the centre of the dry ingredients, pour the yeast mixture into it and sprinkle a little flour over it. Cover and allow to stand in a warm place for a few minutes. Beat the eggs, pour them on the yeast mixture and proceed to knead the ingredients to a soft dough. Melt the treacle in a little warm water and

gradually add it to the dough, as required, when kneading.
Cover the bowl and allow the dough to rise for an hour and a half in a warm place.
Then turn out on to a well-floured board, divide it in equal parts and put into warm greased tins.
Bake the loaves in a moderately hot oven for an hour to an hour and a half.
Bala, Merioneth.

Bara Cyrens—Currant Bread

seven pounds wholemeal flour
one and a half ounces dried yeast
a pinch of salt
one pound currants
a mixture of warm water and milk

Soften the yeast with a little warm water. Work the currants into the flour, make a well in the centre and pour in the yeast mixture. Allow the yeast to become frothy and then proceed to mix the dough by adding the milk and water gradually to give a soft consistency. Knead well and leave to rise in a warm place for an hour. Shape into loaves, put them in greased tins and bake in a hot oven.

This currant bread was baked for special occasions only—to celebrate Christmas and the New Year and for Harvest Home Suppers.
Rhydlewis, Cardiganshire.

Bara Carwe Sir Fôn—
Anglesey Caraway Bread

one pound plain flour
a little baking powder
two and a half ounces butter
one ounce sugar
half an ounce caraway seeds
half a pint milk
a little salt

Rub the fat into the flour, work in the other dry ingredients and gradually add the milk to make a soft dough. Put it into a greased cake tin and bake in a moderately hot oven for approximately one hour.
Beaumaris, Anglesey.

Baking bread in a pot oven. Mrs. Pati John, Mynachlog Ddu, Pembrokeshire.>

Bara Carwe—Caraway Bread

one pound plain flour
a little baking powder
one teaspoonful salt
half a tablespoonful caraway seeds
one ounce sugar
two and a half ounces butter
one egg
quarter pint milk

Sift the flour and salt into a bowl, rub in the butter and
add the other dry ingredients. Beat the egg and milk
together and gradually pour into the dry ingredients,
mixing well to make a light dough. Put this dough into a
greased tin and bake in a moderately hot oven for
approximately one hour.
Aberystwyth, Cardiganshire.

Bara Sinsir—Gingerbread

half a pound plain flour
two teaspoonfuls ground ginger
one teaspoonful mixed spice
two ounces butter
eight tablespoonfuls black treacle or syrup
one ounce soft brown sugar
one egg
quarter pint milk
half a teaspoonful bicarbonate of soda

Melt the treacle, butter and sugar over a low heat.
Sift the flour, ginger, spice and soda into a bowl and
pour in the melted treacle mixture. Beat the egg and
milk together, add them to the other ingredients in the
bowl and mix all together thoroughly.
Grease a shallow cake tin and line with greaseproof
paper. Put the mixture into it, spread evenly and bake in
a moderately hot oven for approximately forty minutes.
Llanybyther, Carmarthenshire.

Bara Sinsir—Gingerbread

three quarter pound plain flour
three ounces butter
two ounces candied peel

half a teaspoonful bicarbonate of soda
one teaspoonful cream of tartar
four teaspoonfuls ground ginger
two eggs, well beaten
six ounces black treacle
six ounces demerara sugar
a little warm milk

Rub the fat into the flour, add the other dry ingredients
and work them into the flour. Dissolve the treacle in the
warm milk, add the beaten eggs and pour this mixture
gradually into the dry ingredients, stirring well with a
wooden spoon. Put the mixture in a greased shallow tin
and bake in a hot oven for approximately one hour.
Allow the cake to cool before cutting it up into squares.

This gingerbread was sold on fair days in Radnorshire.
Llandrindod, Radnorshire.

Gingerbread moulds.

Bara Brau—Shortbread

eight ounces butter
twelve ounces wholemeal flour
four ounces rice flour
eight ounces sugar

Cream the butter until soft, sift the wholemeal flour over it and work it into the butter. Add the sugar and rice flour and knead well to a soft dough.
Divide the dough into four equal parts and shape into flat rounds. Prick the surfaces lightly with a fork and pinch the edge of each one with the thumb and forefinger. Place on a shallow tin and bake in a moderately hot oven for approximately half an hour.

This shortbread was prepared specially for the *noson lawen* (merry evenings) held in the farmhouses in Radnorshire.
Llandrindod, Radnorshire.

Burum Cartref—Home Made Yeast

four ounces hops
six potatoes (unpeeled)
one and a half gallons water
one cupful sugar
one cupful flour
quarter pint yeast reserved from previous lot

Boil the potatoes and hops in the water until the potatoes have disintegrated. Strain the infusion into an earthenware bowl and allow it to cool to blood heat.
Mix the sugar and flour with a small quantity of this liquid, pour it back on to the remainder in the bowl and then add the old yeast. Cover the bowl and allow to stand in a warm place for two days.
Now strain the liquid yeast into bottles or earthenware jars, cork tightly and store in a cool place.
Pennant, Montgomeryshire.

Liquid yeast prepared at home in this way was known as *burum total* or *burum dirwest* (temperance yeast) in Cardiganshire. Its strength was not equal to that of the dried yeast and this accounted for the custom of preparing the dough in the evenings and leaving it to rise in a warm place overnight.
Rhydlewis, Cardiganshire.

Home made liquid yeast was prepared in large quantities to augment the family income. Known as *berman dirwest* or *berman total,* it was sold to the neighbours for approximately a penny per pint. It was also possible to buy liquid yeast *(berman tafarn)* from the local inn; this brewers' yeast proved to be stronger than the home made variety.
Pen-prysg, Glamorgan.

Cereal and Milk Dishes

On interviewing informants in the agricultural areas of Wales regarding their daily menu and food patterns, it soon became evident that the home-grown crop of oats was of considerable value to every farmer. The oatmeal, in turn, was one of the basic ingredients used in many of the dishes consumed regularly by his family. After it had been harvested and threshed by the farmer, the cereal was then taken to the local mill to be dried carefully in the kiln, and then hulled *(silio)* before it was ground to the required degree of fineness.

Informants in south Cardiganshire refer to *cario'r gynnos i'r felin,* namely taking a specific quantity of oats needed for human consumption to the mill, in contrast to that which was ground as fodder for the animals. In some districts, the farmer himself would be responsible for drying the oats in the kiln at the mill and to mark the occasion he would invite his friends to join him there for the evening. They would while away the time singing and holding a kind of *noson lawen* (a merry evening) while the oats were being dried. *Shimli* was the local term given to this particular gathering in Cardiganshire. Hulling the oats was the next step, i.e. separating the kernel *(y pilcornyn* or *y dalchen)* from its shell *(yr eisin* or *y plisgyn).* The oats were fed through the millstones, in this instance, but on no account should the runner and bedstone break up the cereal—the kernel had to be kept intact. This process was repeated, but with the runner stone lifted slightly the second time. Next the kernels were ground and subsequently the meal was sifted, twice, to rid it of any husks or gross meal.

Special oak chests were found in most farmhouses for storing this pure oatmeal. Housed in a warm, dry room, usually in the bedroom above the kitchen, these chests, referred to by Thomas Pennant as *cistiau styffylog,* held the essential part of the household's provision. Bringing home the oatmeal from the mill was a very special occasion in most homes. Members of the family would wear clean, white stockings to stamp and tread the meal as it was put into the chests—men, women and children taking their turn to fulfil this important task to ensure that the meal was packed really tightly. Stored in this way it would keep fresh and free of mites for twelve months or longer.

Oatmeal is the basic ingredient used in many of the dishes included in this chapter.

Llymru—Flummery

one large cupful oatmeal (or flummery meal)
one quart cold water
half a cupful buttermilk

Steep the oatmeal in the cold water and buttermilk for three or four days until the mixture is sour. Then strain through a very fine sieve, extracting all the liquid from the meal. Boil the liquid briskly and stir continuously with a wooden stick or spoon. To test its consistency, hold the stick covered with flummery a few inches above the saucepan and if the mixture seems to form a thin ribbon or 'tail' as it runs back into the pan, it will have boiled to the required degree. Pour the flummery into a dish rinsed beforehand with cold water, and leave to cool. Serve in cold milk or with treacle dissolved in hot water.
Llanuwchllyn, Merioneth.

Preparing flummery. Mrs. Catrin Jones, Bala, Merioneth.

1

Straining all liquid from the steeped oatmeal.

3

Pouring a small quantity into a cast iron saucepan.

2

The flummery liquid before boiling.

4

The liquid forming a thin ribbon or 'tail' as it runs from the tip of the flummery stick.

5

The flummery, when set.

Llymru was served for breakfast or supper, especially during the summer months.
Llangwnadl, Caernarvonshire.

A dish highly recommended for a person suffering from a kidney ailment.
Llanuwchllyn, Merioneth.

The dish known as *llymru* (flummery) in the counties of north Wales is basically the same dish as the one known as *sucan* or *uwd sucan* in south Wales (see *sucan* recipe). A reference to this variation in names is found in the renowned Morris' Letters. In a letter to his brother Richard, Lewis Morris writes in 1760, '. . . toccins yw arian cochion yn sir Faesyfed a sucan neu uwd y gelwir llymru yno' (. . . copper money is known as *toccins* in Radnorshire and *llymru* is called *sucan* or *uwd* there).

The stick used to stir the *llymru* varied slightly in size and form and was known by different names, e.g. *myndl* in Montgomeryshire, *mopran* or *pren llymru* in Caernarvonshire, and *wtffon* or *rhwtffon* in Merioneth.

The following couplets or phrases referring to *llymru* are quoted locally:

'Llymru lled amrwd
I lenwi bol yn lle bwyd.'
Llangybi, Caernarvonshire.
(Raw/crude *llymru*
To fill the belly in place of food)

'Llymru llwyd da i ddim
Ond i lenwi bol rhag isho bwyd.'
Parc, Merioneth.
(Pale *llymru*, good for nothing
But to fill the belly and suppress hunger)

'Cyn llwyted â llymru'
(As pale as *llymru*)

'Croen uwd a chreifion llymru.'
Gwerin Eiriau, Caernarvonshire.
(Porridge skin and *llymru* scrapings)

Sucan—Sowans

one large cupful *sucan* meal
one and a half pints cold water

Leave the *sucan* meal to steep in the cold water overnight. Pour the mixture through a fine sieve, squeezing the meal between the hands to extract all the liquid. Put this liquid in a saucepan and bring to the boil, stirring it continuously with a wooden stick or spoon. When the mixture forms a thin ribbon or 'tail' when dropped from the tip of the stick held above the saucepan, it has boiled to the required consistency. Pour the *sucan* into a bowl, rinsed beforehand with cold water and leave to set.
Serve in cold milk.
Pren-gwyn, Cardiganshire.

This dish was known as *uwd* or *uwd sucan* in south Cardiganshire and north Pembrokeshire, e.g.
Pren-gwyn, Cardiganshire.
Brynberian, Pembrokeshire.

Sucan was associated with the hay harvest in many areas. Boiled in large quantities, it was carried out to the field in tin pans and served to the helpers at mid-day.

The local observations given in connection with testing the consistency of the *sucan* are noteworthy, e.g. *rhaid iddo ffurfio rheffyn fel cwt cath* (it must form a ribbon like a cat's tail) (Croes-lan, Cardiganshire), or *rhaid i'r sucan ddisgyn o'r pren fel cwt buwch* (the *sucan* must drop from the stick like a cow's tail) (Llandysul, Cardiganshire), or *yr uwd yn berwi fel llygad eidion* (the *uwd* boiling like a bullock's eye) (Brynhoffnant, Cardiganshire).

Particular attention was paid to the surface of the *sucan* when set; a smooth surface without a single crack in it was a sure proof of the cook's expertise at preparing the dish, but the unsuccessful cook had to face the mockery of the old belief that a cracked surface signified that she would marry a boy with an ugly face.

Blawd sucan—Sucan meal
The method of preparing this oatmeal by-product varied slightly in different areas. The following process was described by one experienced miller. After the oats had been dried and hulled, the kernels were crushed finely. This meal was then sifted to rid it of any husks or gross meal and the material that was left on the sieve (i.e. a mixture of gross meal and oat husks) was known as *blawd* (meal) or *bwyd* (food) *sucan*.
Crug-y-bar, Carmarthenshire.

Sucan Gwyn—White Sowans

one large cupful oatmeal
one quart cold water
half a cupful buttermilk
one pint cold water
a little sugar and ginger

Leave the oatmeal to steep in the quart of cold water and buttermilk for two nights until soured. Then pour off the surface water and pour two tablespoonfuls of the mixture through a fine sieve. Add to it the pint of cold water, flavour with a little sugar and ginger, and boil for about ten minutes. It should be as thin as milk after boiling.
The remainder of the mixture may be kept fresh for a few days by draining the surface water and replacing it with fresh water.
Mynytho, Caernarvonshire.

Uwd Blawd Ceirch—Oatmeal Porridge

oatmeal
cold water
salt

Bring the salted water to the boil. Then add the dry oatmeal, steadily, and at the very same time, with the other hand, stir the mixture with a wooden spoon. (This prevents the meal from becoming lumpy.) Continue to add oatmeal until the mixture begins to thicken. Boil the porridge slowly and steadily for some time, stirring it occasionally.

Serve with milk or buttermilk.
Mynytho, Lleyn.

Add half a cupful of rice to make the porridge lighter in consistency.
Llanuwchllyn, Merioneth.

The menservants in Lleyn, Caernarvonshire, and in many other districts in north Wales were given *uwd* for supper regularly every night. The cauldron was placed on a wooden stand in the centre of the table and the men were expected to help themselves.
Uwchmynydd, Lleyn.

A porridge that had not been boiled for a sufficient length of time was frowned upon by the servants and was termed *uwd amrwd* (raw porridge). To be on the safe side, the porridge was prepared immediately after the afternoon tea and left to simmer for two to three hours over a low fire. The following couplets are often quoted to describe the nature of the fire in this context:

> 'Tân llym o dan y llymru
> Tân mall wna'r uwd yn well.'

> (A sharp fire beneath the *llymru*
> A smouldering fire improves the *uwd*)

> 'Freshdân dan llymru
> Moed-dân dan uwd.'

> (A fresh fire beneath the *llymru*
> A quiet fire beneath the *uwd*)

Dyffryn Ardudwy and Rhydymain, Merioneth.

Crushing an oatcake with a wooden crusher.

1

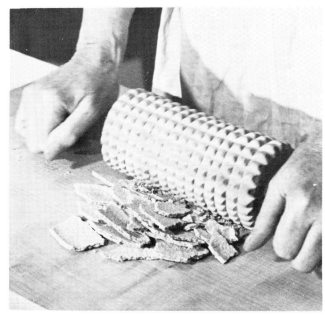

3

Preparing shot. Mrs. Catrin Jones, Bala, Merioneth.

2

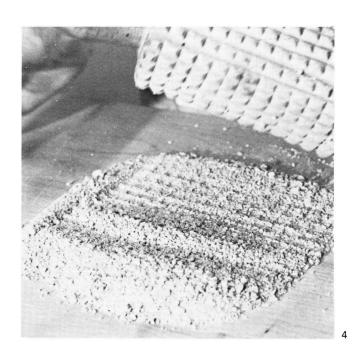

4

Llith—Oatmeal and Buttermilk

three tablespoonfuls oatmeal
cold buttermilk

Put the oatmeal in a basin or bowl and fill it with
buttermilk. Stir well and eat immediately.

A popular dish during harvest time, it was usually eaten
as a snack between meals.
Rhydlewis, Cardiganshire.

This dish was known as *sopas* in parts of Pembrokeshire,
e.g. *Trefdraeth, Pembrokeshire.*

Siot—Shot

a thick oatcake (without fat)
cold buttermilk

Crush the oatcake finely and put in a bowl or basin.
Add to it cold buttermilk, stir well and serve
immediately. Alternatively, leave the mixture to stand for
about an hour and add more buttermilk when serving,
if desired.

A popular dish served for afternoon tea during the
summer months, regarded by many as an ideal thirst
quencher.
Llanuwchllyn, Merioneth.

Siot was a dish suitable for carrying out as a snack for
the workers during harvest time. Children would also
carry it to school in cans for their mid-day meal.
Prion, Denbighshire.

The following variations of the basic dish were also
prepared:—
Siot gynnes—pour warm buttermilk over the crushed
oatcake.
Siot bosel—pour warm milk over the crushed oatcake
and add a little cold buttermilk before serving.
Siot faidd—add whey to the crushed oatcake instead
of the usual buttermilk.
Parc, Merioneth.

Picws Mali was the name given to the basic dish in some
areas in north Wales, e.g.
Mynytho, Caernarvonshire.

The crushed oatcake placed in individual bowls.

5

Adding cold buttermilk to it.

6

Gooseblood tart, a Christmas delicacy in parts of Montgomeryshire. >

Brŵes Bara Ceirch—Oatcake Brewis

one oatcake (prepared without fat)
beef stock
pepper and salt

Crush the oatcake finely and put in a bowl or basin.
Pour boiling stock over it and add pepper and salt to
taste. Leave to steep for a few minutes before serving.
Uwchmynydd, Lleyn.

Brŵes was served regularly for breakfast on Wednesdays
and Sundays on the Lleyn peninsula.

A little beef dripping and boiling water were used as
alternatives to the stock, but the dish was then termed
brŵes trodnoeth (barefooted brewis) or *brŵes pig tegell*
(kettle-spout brewis).
Dyffryn Ardudwy, Merioneth.

Cawl Llaeth—Milk Broth

approximately one pint skim-milk
one tablespoonful oatmeal
a little cold water
a pinch of salt

Pour the skim-milk into a saucepan and bring it to the
boil. Blend the oatmeal with cold water and pour it into
the milk when boiling. Add a little salt, stir and bring it
back to the boil.

A dish served for breakfast or supper, usually.
Rhydlewis, Cardiganshire.

Known as *potes llaeth* in Anglesey, it was served with
pieces of bread broken into it.
Llanfachraeth, Anglesey.

Twym llaeth was the name given to the same dish in
parts of Carmarthenshire.
Caeo, Carmarthenshire.

Griwel Blawd Ceirch—Oatmeal Gruel

oatmeal
cold water
cold milk
salt
sugar

Put a quantity of oatmeal in an earthenware crock, cover
with cold water and leave to stand overnight. Strain, and
bring the liquid to the boil. Pour in the milk and add the
sugar and salt to taste. Re-boil for a further few minutes.
or
Work the oatmeal through a fine sieve, pour cold milk
over it and boil for about ten minutes, adding salt and
sugar to taste.
Dyffryn Ardudwy, Merioneth.

A light, nourishing dish, served mainly as an invalid food.
It was also given to the mother of a new-born baby as it
was considered to have certain qualities to help her
produce milk for the infant.
Upper Banwy, Montgomeryshire.

Bwdram—Thin Flummery

one large cupful *sucan* meal (or oatmeal)
one quart tepid water

Steep the meal in the water overnight. Strain through a
very fine sieve and add a little water if the mixture is too
thick. Boil, stirring continuously, for about five minutes.
Pour over pieces of bread in a bowl.
Rhydlewis, Cardiganshire.

Bwdram was generally served for supper in some districts
and it is known that *bwdram a sgadan* (*bwdram* and
fresh herrings) was a popular combination, deemed a
luxury in the coastal areas of Cardiganshire.
Brynhoffnant, Cardiganshire.

Flavoured with sugar, ginger and a little butter, this dish
was given to the mother of a new-born baby owing to its
medicinal qualities.
Cwm-bach, Carmarthenshire.

Sgotyn—Bread in Water

bread
salt and pepper
boiling water

Break a slice of bread into a bowl, pour boiling water over
it and add salt and pepper, to taste.
Serve immediately.
Dyffryn Ardudwy, Merioneth.

Substitute a knob of butter and a little sugar for the salt and pepper and prepare the dish as above.
Llanfachraeth, Anglesey.

Bara Llaeth Wedi'i Grasu— Toasted Bread in Buttermilk

a thick slice of bread
cold buttermilk

Toast a thick slice of bread and break it into a bowl. Pour cold buttermilk over it and allow to steep for about an hour before serving.
Dyffryn Ardudwy, Merioneth.

Toast a thick slice of bread, break it into a bowl and pour cold buttermilk over it. Cover the bowl with a plate or a saucer and put it in a warm oven. Allow the toast to take in the buttermilk before serving.
Llanfachraeth, Anglesey.

Although served only during very hot spells in some districts, it was a dish eaten regularly for supper all through the summer in other areas. It would be also carried in 'cans' and served as a snack to the harvesters out on the fields, e.g.
Dyffryn Ardudwy, Merioneth.

Bara Llefrith—Bread and Milk

one slice of wholewheat bread per person
milk
sugar or salt

Break the bread into small pieces and put in a large saucepan. Cover with milk and bring to the boil. Serve in bowls and add sugar or salt, to taste.
or
Break the bread into individual bowls and cover with boiling milk. Add sugar or salt, to taste.

A dish commonly served for breakfast or afternoon tea.
Dyffryn Ardudwy, Merioneth.

Posel Llaeth neu Ddeulaeth—Milk Posset

one quart buttermilk
one quart fresh milk

Put the cold buttermilk in a large bowl and quickly pour into it the fresh milk, boiling hot. This will cause the two different milks to turn into curds and whey.
Llanfachraeth, Anglesey.

The above dish, flavoured with ginger was taken as an antidote to the common cold shortly before retiring to bed.
Pennant, Montgomeryshire.

Treacle was sometimes added to the above dish, which was then termed *posel triog* (treacle posset).
Dyffryn Ardudwy, Merioneth.

Maidd yr Iâr—Egg Whey

a thick slice of bread
one or two eggs
half a pint of milk
a little nutmeg, ginger and sugar

Break the bread into a saucepan, whisk the eggs and pour over the bread together with the milk. Add the nutmeg, ginger and sugar to taste. Heat the mixture over a low flame but do *not* boil. Alternatively put the mixture in a dish and bake in a moderately hot oven.
Holyhead, Anglesey.

Heat the milk in a saucepan but do not boil. Break the bread into a bowl, and pour the eggs, well beaten, and the hot milk over it. Add sugar or salt, to taste. Cover the bowl with a plate and leave to stand for a few minutes before serving.
Llanfachraeth, Anglesey.

Pastai Dwrci—Turkey Pie

a thick slice of bread
boiling water
a knob of butter
salt and pepper

Put the bread in a bowl and cover with boiling water. Lift out the bread and squeeze the excess water out of it. Put the sodden bread in another bowl, work the butter into it and add salt and pepper to taste. Pack the mixture tightly in a cup and then turn out on a plate. Serve while warm.
Llanfachraeth, Anglesey.

Siencyn—Bread and Water

boiling water
a slice of bread
a knob of butter or dripping
salt and pepper

Break the bread into a basin and cover with boiling water.
Add the fat, and season with salt and pepper.
A dish served generally for breakfast.
Upper Banwy, Montgomeryshire.

Siencyn Te (Bread and Tea)

Add hot tea instead of the boiling water, sweeten the dish with sugar and top with a little cold milk.

Siencyn and a lump of cheese was regarded as a nutritious meal served regularly for breakfast or supper in the industrial valleys of south Wales.
Dowlais, Glamorgan.

Sop was the term given to the same dish in other districts in south Wales.
Ystalyfera, Glamorgan.

Puddings

Pwdin Nadolig—Christmas Pudding

half a pound plain flour
half a pound bread-crumbs
half a pound brown sugar
six ounces suet
one pound currants
one pound sultanas
one pound raisins
four to six eggs, well beaten
a little milk or beer
the rind of one lemon (grated)
one large apple (diced)

Rub the suet into the flour, add the other dry
ingredients and work them into the mixture. Pour in the
beaten eggs, stir with a wooden spoon, and gradually add
milk or beer to make a fairly stiff consistency. Put into
greased earthenware basins, cover with a layer of
greaseproof paper and a clean cloth and tie securely.
Stand the basins in water in a large saucepan and boil
for about seven hours, keeping the level of the water
just below the edge of the basins.
When required, re-boil for about two hours, slice, and
serve with white sauce.

Mixing the Christmas pudding involved the whole family
when each member, from the youngest to the oldest,
would take his turn to stir the pudding and in doing so
would cast a secret wish. It was a common custom also
when preparing the pudding to put small coins in the
mixture—the old silver threepenny or sixpenny pieces,
and the lucky recipients on Christmas day regarded them
as tokens of good luck.
Dowlais, Glamorgan.

Pwdin Lwmp—Christmas Pudding

one basinful plain flour
one basinful suet
one basinful currants
one basinful sugar
one basinful candied peel
a little salt
one tablespoonful treacle
one or two eggs, well beaten
warm buttermilk
one teaspoonful bicarbonate of soda

Dice the suet finely and work it into the flour. Add all
the other dry ingredients and mix thoroughly. Pour the
eggs into a hole in the centre of this dry mixture.
Dissolve the treacle and soda in the warm buttermilk
and add gradually to the other ingredients to give a
moist consistency, stirring well with a wooden spoon.
Put the mixture into greased bowls, cover with
greaseproof paper and clean cloths, and tie securely.
Boil in the usual way for four or five hours.
Mynytho, Caernarvonshire.

The old traditional method was to boil the mixture in one
large lump in a linen bag—the custom that gave it the
names—*pwdin lwmp* (lump pudding), *pwdin clwt* (rag
pudding) or *pwdin cwd* (bag pudding). The mixture was
placed on a large damp cloth, the edges of which were
then bunched together and tied securely with strong cord
to form a bag. This bag was then suspended from a stick
placed across the top of the boiler or cauldron and
immersed in boiling water.

This pudding was prepared for dinner on corn threshing day on the farms, as well as for Christmas day. As a second course on threshing day, it was served with warm rice pudding, whereas it was served with *menyn melys* (sweet butter) on Christmas day.

Saws Gwyn—White Sauce

half a pint milk
approximately one cupful cold water
approximately two dessertspoonfuls plain flour
(or cornflour)
a little sugar
a pinch of salt
a little rum (optional)

Blend the flour with a little of the milk. Heat the water and the remainder of the milk in a saucepan and pour the flour mixture into it. Add salt, sugar and rum to taste, and then bring to the boil, stirring continuously.
Serve hot, with Christmas pudding.
Dowlais, Glamorgan.

Menyn melys (sweet butter) is the name given to this sauce in many districts in north Wales.
Uwch-mynydd, Lleyn.

Pwdin Reis—Rice Pudding

one cupful rice
one cupful sugar
four pints milk
a pinch of salt
a little nutmeg

Put the rice in a large dish and barely cover with cold water. Place it in a moderately hot oven and allow the water to evaporate. Then pour the milk over it and add the sugar and salt. Stir well and finally add a little ground nutmeg. Bake in a moderately hot oven until it becomes thick and creamy. (Beaten eggs may be added if a richer consistency is required.)
Pennant, Montgomeryshire.

This was the pudding most commonly eaten for Sunday dinner throughout Wales. A large bowlful would also be prepared periodically on a week-day. After baking bread in the large brick oven, the housewife would make use of the heat still retained by the bricks, by putting a large bowlful of rice pudding to bake slowly in the oven overnight.
Alternatively, rice pudding was boiled in a cast iron saucepan or boiler over an open fire.

Pwdin Reis—Rice Pudding

one pound rice
one gallon milk
one pound currants
one pound raisins
half a pound brown sugar
one dozen eggs

Following the usual method, bake the pudding slowly, until it reaches the same consistency as a cake. When cool, cut into squares and serve cold.
Margam, Glamorgan.

During the hay and corn harvests in the Vale of Glamorgan this particular rice pudding was baked in large tin pans and carried out to the workers in the fields.

Pwdin Mari Morris—
Mary Morris' Pudding

rice
salt
water
currants (optional)

Wash the rice and put it in a linen bag. Sprinkle with salt and add currants. Secure the bag tightly and keep it immersed in boiling water for two hours.
Serve with sugar and cold milk.
Dyffryn Ardudwy, Merioneth.

Pwdin Bara—Bread Pudding

eight ounces stale bread
cold water
two eggs, well beaten
a little milk

two ounces brown sugar
four ounces sultanas or currants
nutmeg, optional

Soak the bread in cold water overnight (cold tea or cold milk may be used as alternatives to water).
Squeeze the bread to remove excess liquid and then add the eggs, brown sugar, fruit and a little milk. Beat well to give a fairly stiff consistency. Add a little nutmeg, if desired.
Put the mixture in a greased, shallow tin, place a few knobs of butter on top and bake it in a moderately hot oven for about an hour.
When cold, cut into squares and eat as cake.

By adding more milk to this mixture a softer pudding may be prepared.
Dowlais, Glamorgan.

In order to augment the family income housewives in the coal-mining valleys would prepare this bread-pudding cake in large quantities and sell it from their homes or in the local markets, e.g. at
Cwm-aman, Aberdare, Glamorgan.

Pwdin Pancos—Pancake Pudding

short-crust pastry
sultanas
one pint sweetened batter (see pancake mixture)
a little butter

Line a pie dish with the pastry and cover it with a layer of sultanas. Then pour in the batter mixture and dot it with butter. Bake in a moderately hot oven for about one hour.

Generally, this pudding, prepared in greater quantities, would be baked along with the bread in the wall oven.
Llandeilo, Carmarthenshire.

Twmplins Afalau—Apple Dumplings

apples—one per person
short-crust pastry

Roll out the prepared pastry fairly thinly and cut into squares according to the size of the apples.

Wash the apples but do not peel them. Wrap a square of pastry around each apple to form a second skin and immerse gently in a saucepanful of boiling water. Continue to boil until small cracks appear on the surface of the pastry. At this point the apples should be thoroughly cooked.
Lift each dumpling out of the water carefully and drain. Serve, while hot, with brown sugar and cold milk.
Pen-prysg, Glamorgan.

Dumplings were boiled together with the meat and vegetables in the broth in many districts. Fat rising to the surface of the broth would be skimmed and put into the pastry instead of lard. To prevent the pastry from disintegrating, it was imperative that the broth was boiling when the dumplings were immersed in it.

Twmplen Gwsberis—Gooseberry Dumpling

short-crust pastry
gooseberries

Line a greased pudding basin with pastry, fill it with gooseberries and cover them with another layer of pastry. Seal the two layers of pastry along the top edge of the basin, cover with a clean cloth and tie securely. Stand the basin in a saucepan, half full of water, and boil for approximately one hour.
Serve while warm and add sugar to taste, together with a little cold milk, if desired.
Groes-goch, Pembrokeshire.

Twmplen—Suet Dumpling

one and a half pounds plain flour
half a pound lard or dripping (or suet)
half a teaspoonful salt
half a teaspoonful bicarbonate of soda
half a pint buttermilk
jam or fresh fruit

Rub the fat into the flour and add the salt. Dissolve the soda in the buttermilk, and pour it gradually into the flour to make a light pastry mixture.
Roll out to an oblong shape, line with fresh fruit (rhubarb, gooseberries, etc.) and fold over tightly.

Cover the dumpling with a damp cloth and tie securely at both ends. Immerse in boiling water and boil for an hour and a half. Slice the dumpling and serve hot with sugar, and a little cold milk if desired.
Pennant, Montgomeryshire.

Suet dumpling was prepared regularly for the mid-day meal in parts of Montgomeryshire. At one time it was general custom to give it as first course to take the edge off the appetite of the menfolk before serving them with meat and vegetables.
If fresh fruit was not available, it was possible to boil a plain dumpling which would be known as *tymplen ddall* (a blind dumpling). It was then served with jam or treacle.

This pudding was known as *pwdin berwi* (boiled pudding) or *pwdin siwet* (suet pudding) in parts of Caernarvonshire.
Mynytho, Lleyn.

Pwdin Berwi—Boiled Pudding

plain flour
salt
sugar
currants
a little suet
bicarbonate of soda
boiling water
buttermilk
(Quantities were measured by rule of thumb)

Put all the dry ingredients in a bowl. Dissolve the soda in the warm water and allow to cool before adding the buttermilk to it. Pour this liquid gradually into the dry ingredients and stir well with a wooden spoon.
Put the mixture in a linen cloth, tie securely and immerse in boiling water. Boil for approximately two hours.

Slice and serve with white sauce.
Dyffryn Ardudwy, Merioneth.

Pwdin Berwi—Boiled Pudding

six ounces plain flour
two ounces sugar
two ounces fat (butter or lard)

half a pint hot milk
one teaspoonful ginger
half a teaspoonful bicarbonate of soda
dried fruit, if desired

Melt the fat in the hot milk and pour gradually into the dry ingredients. Mix together well and put the mixture in a greased basin. Cover with greaseproof paper or cloth, tie securely and stand the basin in a saucepan half full of water. Boil for approximately one and a half hours.

This pudding was served, fairly regularly, as a second course for the mid-day meal during the winter months in the Gower area.
Gower Peninsula.

Pwdin Modryb Martha—Aunt Martha's Pudding

five ounces bread-crumbs
one egg, well beaten
two ounces butter
two ounces sugar
one lemon
one cupful milk
quarter pound raisins
nutmeg

Boil the milk and pour it over the sugar and bread-crumbs. Then add the beaten egg, the rind and juice of the lemon, the butter and the nutmeg. Beat well for several minutes. Grease a pudding basin thickly with butter, dot the raisins in this butter layer and pour the mixture into the basin. Stand the basin in a saucepan with boiling water and boil for approximately one and a half hours.

This pudding, being inexpensive to prepare, was eaten fairly regularly by the thrifty families.
Gower Peninsula.

Dowset

short-crust pastry
two large eggs, well beaten
half a pint milk

one dessertspoonful plain flour
a little salt
a little nutmeg
two tablespoonfuls sugar

Blend the flour with a little of the milk and then pour it
into the remainder of the milk and the beaten eggs. Add
the sugar and salt, and beat well.
Line a deep pie dish with a layer of pastry, pour the
prepared mixture into it and sprinkle the ground nutmeg
on top.
Bake in a moderately hot oven for about half an hour, or
until the mixture is set.
Gower Peninsula.

Dowset

short-crust pastry
six tablespoonfuls plain flour
half a teaspoonful baking powder
two teaspoonfuls sugar
a pinch of salt
one egg, well beaten
jam

Line a pie dish with a thin layer of pastry and spread
jam on it. Put the dry ingredients in a bowl and gradually
add the beaten egg to make a smooth batter. Pour this
mixture over the jam and bake the pudding in a fairly
hot oven until golden brown.

Generally on bread baking day, the farmers' wives would
bake a large tinful of this pudding in the wall oven and
keep it for the family's Saturday dinner. Saturday
morning was usually taken up with cleaning the house
and they did not have time to prepare a cooked
mid-day meal.
Gower Peninsula.

Pwdin Mamgu—Grandmother's Pudding

eight ounces stale bread-crumbs
two ounces shredded suet
threequarter pound blackberries
threequarter pound apples, sliced
three ounces sugar
half a pint milk

Soak the bread-crumbs in the milk, add the suet and
mix well. Place a layer of this mixture on the bottom of
a well-greased pie dish, and cover with a layer of
blackberries and apple. Continue to fill the dish with
alternate layers of bread-crumb mixture and fruit, the
final one being a thick layer of the bread-crumb mixture.
Bake in a moderately hot oven for approximately one
hour until golden brown.
Gower Peninsula.

Trolis Blawd Plaen—Plain Flour Trollies

six ounces plain flour
two ounces suet
two ounces currants
a pinch of salt
milk

Shred the suet finely and work into the flour together
with the other dry ingredients. Bind with a little milk to
make a stiff dough.
Divide the dough into four or six equal parts and form
into medium size balls. Drop gently into boiling water
and boil for some twenty minutes.
Serve hot with brown sugar.
Llanelli, Carmarthenshire.

Mwyar Duon—Blackberry Pudding

a large, thick slice of white bread
blackberries
sugar
a little water
fresh cream

Put the slice of bread at the bottom of a pie dish.
Simmer the blackberries in a little water, with sugar
added to taste. When soft, pour the stewed fruit over
the bread and leave to cool. Finally, top with fresh
cream.
Carmarthen.

Whipod—White pot

half a cupful rice
half a pint boiling milk
quarter teaspoonful salt
one tablespoonful sugar

*An ingle-nook fireplace, featuring a built-in wall oven and crane
at Blaenau, Farmers, Carmarthenshire.* >

one teaspoonful butter
one egg, well beaten
shredded rind of one lemon

Soak the rice in warm water for three hours. Drain, put the rice in a saucepan and pour the boiling milk over it. Boil for half an hour and then add the sugar, butter and salt. Simmer for another ten minutes and then allow to cool before pouring the egg slowly into the mixture. Finally add the lemon rind. Stir, bring to the boil once more, and continue to boil until the mixture thickens.
Gower Peninsula.

Whipod—White pot

two tablespoonfuls plain flour
two tablespoonfuls sugar
one pint milk
two ounces currants
a little salt
large knob of butter
a little nutmeg
one ounce candied peel

Blend the flour with a little of the milk. Heat the remainder of the milk, and when on the point of boiling, pour it over the flour mixture and stir well. Now add the other dry ingredients, pour the mixture back into the saucepan and boil for some fifteen to twenty minutes. This pudding should be served warm at all times.

White pot was associated with the corn harvest on the farms of the Gower peninsula. It was served as a part of the workmen's lunch in the fields or with bread and butter for their supper.
Gower Peninsula.

Pwdin Llaeth Brith—Beestings Pudding

milk taken from the second or third milking after the cow has given birth to a calf
sugar
salt
ginger (or currants, if preferable)

Pour the milk into a dish, add the sugar, salt and ginger to taste and bake in a hot oven until the mixture has thickened. (A little ordinary milk may be added to prevent the pudding from becoming too thick.)

or

Add sugar, salt and ginger to the milk and pour into a jug or a tall container. Cover it and put it to stand in a saucepan of water. Bring the water to the boil and allow the mixture to thicken slowly in this heat.
Dyffryn Ardudwy, Merioneth.

The names given to this pudding and the methods of preparing it varied considerably in different districts. Similar in consistency to egg custard, it was eaten quite regularly in many areas. *Pwdin llo bach* (calf pudding) was a common name given to it in the counties of Denbigh and Merioneth, but it was known as *pwdin llaeth tor* in Anglesey.

Pwdin Llaeth Brith—Beestings Pudding

'new' milk taken from the second milking after a cow has calved
warm water
sugar
salt
a little ground nutmeg

Half fill a pudding dish with warm water and dissolve the sugar and salt in it. Then fill the remainder of the dish with the 'new' milk. Sprinkle with a little nutmeg and bake slowly in a cool oven.
Rhydymain, Merioneth.

Fish

Bara Lawr—Laverbread

laver (porphyra laciniata)
salt
oatmeal

Wash the laver well in cold water, put it in a large saucepan and simmer for several hours. (It is *not* necessary to add water as the leaves themselves contain sufficient moisture.)
When soft, drain the leaves thoroughly, chop finely with a sharp knife and add salt to taste. Form mixture into small balls and roll in oatmeal.
Rhydlewis, Cardiganshire.

Boil the leaves in a little water and vinegar for about two hours.
South Pembrokeshire.

The most common method of cooking laverbread in the counties of south Wales was to fry it in bacon fat and serve it with bacon, usually for breakfast.

Llymrîaid—Sand eels

approximately one quart sand eels
bacon fat

Wash the sand eels thoroughly, cut off their heads and squeeze out their entrails. Fry them in bacon fat together with a sliced onion, if desired.

Prepared in this way, they were usually served for lunch or for supper.
Nefyn, Lleyn.

It was not an uncommon sight to see whole families burrowing on the beaches on a moonlit night during the summer months, looking for sand eels. The old custom of *llymreita* (collecting sand eels) was practised generally during the small hours of the first night of the ebb tide. Working in teams of two or three, spades or sickles were used to burrow in the sand, and the eels, when exposed, were quickly caught and put into buckets or cans.
Pen-bryn, Cardiganshire.

Gwichiaid—Periwinkles

approximately a quart of periwinkles
salt water

When thoroughly washed, put the winkles in a saucepan, cover with salt water and bring to the boil. When boiling point is reached, remove the saucepan from the heat and allow the winkles to cool in this water. (Boiling the winkles causes them to become tough.) When cold, drain the winkles, take them out of their shells, season with salt and pepper and serve at once.
Aberdaron, Lleyn.

Boil the winkles in salt water for about half an hour until the winkles begin to leave their shells. Drain them, take all the winkles out of their shells, and fry in bacon fat. Finally, crack an egg or two over the winkles and fry

them whole or scramble the eggs with a wooden spoon, mixing the winkles in with them.
Nefyn and Bardsey Island.

The older generation had an unwritten rule that winkles should not be eaten if the letter 'r' was not incorporated in the name of the month in English (i.e. May—August). The winkles were found under stones or seaweed on the beach after high tide.

Llygaid Meheryn—Limpets

limpets
tips of nettle leaves
salt water

Boil the limpets in salt water for a considerable period. (Adding the tips of nettle leaves helps to make the limpets tender.) Take the limpets out of their shells, wash them well and then cut them into quarters. Toss them in oatmeal, and fry in bacon fat.
Pen-bryn, Cardiganshire.

Fry the limpets in bacon fat together with eggs and sliced onions.
Uwchmynydd, Lleyn.

Llygaid y graig is the Welsh name for these particular shell fish in some districts, e.g.
Aber-porth, Cardiganshire.

Tradition has it that limpets were collected only when the letter 'r' appeared in the name of the month in English. They are found clinging to the rocks along the sea shore, and experienced collectors relate that to free them from the rock is quite a difficult task; levering them suddenly with the blade of a knife is one of the surest methods. The limpet itself, housed in a large shell, is comparatively small and has to be collected in large numbers to provide a meal for an average-sized family.

Tarten Lygaid—Limpet Pie

limpets
fatty bacon (diced)
a large leek (the white part only)
short-crust pastry

Boil the limpets for about half an hour, drain them and take them out of their shells. Wash them well and cut into quarters.
Line a deep pie dish with a layer of pastry, cover with the limpets and place the diced bacon and the leek, cut into one inch pieces, over them. Sprinkle with salt and pepper and cover with a second layer of pastry. Seal the pie around the edge of the dish and bake in a hot oven for the first half hour, but reducing the heat for the second half hour.

This pie was served warm, generally for dinner or supper.
Aber-porth, Cardiganshire.

Rhython—Cockles

approximately one quart cockles (shelled)
milk
chives or parsley, finely chopped
salt
flour

Boil the cockles in a reasonable quantity of milk, add the chives or parsley and season with salt. Blend a little flour with cold milk, pour it gradually into the boiling mixture, stir well and bring to the boil again.

Cockle-gathering on Llan-saint beach. Mrs. Lettice Rees, Llan-saint, Carmarthenshire. (Photograph by permission of Miss Margaret Brentnall, Highgate, London.)

Cockle-gathering tools—a large sieve, a rake and cocses *(a bent sickle blade). (Photograph by permission of* Y Cymro.)

This thick 'sauce' was usually served with bread and butter.
Garnant, Carmarthenshire.

Women would go from door to door in many villages in south Wales, selling cockles. Cockles already boiled and taken out of their shells were carried in a wooden pail balanced on the seller's head. These cockles were known as *cocs rhython.* The untreated cockles, still in their shells, were carried in a large basket on the arm and were known as *cocs cregin.* The former were sold for about nine pence per pint and the latter for about sixpence per pint.

Cocos ac Wyau—Cockles and Eggs

approximately one quart cockles (in their shells)
two or three eggs, well beaten
bacon fat
black pepper

Cover the cockles with water and bring to the boil. Boil the cockles for a few minutes only. (Boiling for a long period causes them to become tough.)
Take the cockles out of their shells, wash them well and lay them out on a large cloth to remove excess moisture. Fry them in a little bacon fat, tossing them well in the fat before pouring the beaten eggs over them. Stir well with a wooden spoon and season with black pepper.
Cricieth, Caernarvonshire.

This cockle and egg mixture was eaten between slices of barley bread or oatcakes in the district around Porthmadog, and it was regarded as a luxury there.
In the past, women would walk from Penrhyndeudraeth to Porthmadog to sell cockles. They would knock on doors, dancing and singing the following rhyme:

> Cocos a wya
> Bara cerch tena
> Merched y Penrhyn
> Yn ysgwyd 'u tina!'

> (Cockles and eggs
> Thin oat cakes,
> The girls of Penrhyn
> Doing the shakes!)

Pastai Gocos—Cockle Pie

cockles
salt water
a little oatmeal
salt and pepper
white sauce (unsweetened)
cheese or short-crust pastry

Soak the cockles in salt water overnight, adding a little oatmeal to the water. (The oatmeal helps to clean the cockles.)
Then boil the cockles in clean water until the shells open. Take out of their shells, put in a pie dish, season with salt and pepper and pour the white sauce over them. Cover the sauce with a thick layer of grated cheese or with short-crust pastry. Bake in a hot oven until golden brown.
South Pembrokeshire.

Crancod a Chimychiaid— Crabs and Lobsters

crabs or lobsters
salt water

Immerse the crab or lobster in boiling, salt water and boil, allowing approximately twenty minutes per pound in weight. Allow to cool, take the flesh out of the shell and season with pepper and salt.

Local fishermen at the seaside villages would boil the crabs and lobsters in this way and sell them in their shells to visitors. They were not eaten by the local people in large quantities, but regarded as an important source of income.
Nefyn, Lleyn.

Pennog Ffres—Fresh Herrings

fresh herring
bacon fat

Clean the herring in the usual way, and fry in bacon fat until crisp on both sides.

Usually, herrings were served with potatoes, boiled in their jackets, for a mid-day meal.
Nefyn, Lleyn.

Fried fresh herrings and onions were served for tea or supper.
Nefyn, Lleyn.

Bwdram a sgadan (thin flummery and fresh herrings) was a favourite dish in parts of south Cardiganshire, e.g. *Brynhoffnant, Cardiganshire.*

Sgadenyn is the Welsh equivalent of 'herring' in the counties of south Wales, but *pennog* is the equivalent used in the counties of north Wales. Catching and selling herrings was a major industry in most seaside villages during the autumn months. Fresh herrings would be sold from door to door in the villages themselves and also they would be carried by horse and cart to the adjacent rural areas. Selling them for about a penny each or seven for sixpence, the seller would announce his arrival by crying out a slogan, e.g.

'Sgadan Aberporth
Dau fola ac un corff.'

(Aberporth herrings,
two bellies in one body)

'Sgadan Aberporth
Dau enaid mewn un corff'

(Aberporth herrings,
two souls in one body)

'Penwaig Nefyn, penwaig Nefyn
'U cefna fel cefna hen ffarmwrs
A'u bolia fel bolia tafarnwrs—penwaig ffres!'

(Nefyn herrings, Nefyn herrings,
Backs like backs of old farmers
Bellies like the bellies of inn-keepers—fresh herrings!)

Pennog Picl—Pickled Herrings

six fresh herrings
one teaspoonful pickling spice
one pint vinegar
onion rings
a little salt
quarter pint cold water (approximately)
one teaspoonful black treacle
a little cornflour

Put the herrings (split open and cleaned in the usual way) in an earthenware dish and cover with the vinegar and water. Add to them the spice, salt and onions. Dissolve the treacle in a little warm water and pour it over the herrings. Blend the cornflour with cold water and add it to the liquid in the dish. Bake in a slow oven until the bones have distintegrated.

Pickled herrings and baked jacket potatoes made a delicious meal for dinner or supper.
Nefyn, Lleyn.

Halltu Penwaig—Salting Fresh Herrings

Herrings were usually preserved in salt towards the end of November when the quality of the fish was at its best. The process of salting them varied a little from district

to district, but basically it followed a similar pattern:
Take about a dozen fresh herrings, and split them open.
Remove their entrails, clean them thoroughly and put
them in a large earthenware dish. Cover them with salt,
tossing and turning them in it at regular intervals for
about one hour. When it has absorbed sufficient salt,
the herring becomes pliable, so that it is possible to
bend it, head to tail. Treat some three or four dozen
herrings in this way. Put a thick bed of salt at the
bottom of a wooden cask or tub, lay the herrings tightly,
side by side and head to tail on the salt, and cover them
with another layer of salt. Continue to arrange them in
alternate layers until all the fish are well covered with
salt. Leave for some nine days until the salt has turned
to brine. Then lift the herrings out of the brine, wash and
drain them well.
Re-arrange the herrings in layers in a clean tub.
Dissolve sufficient salt in boiling water so that an egg
will float in it and pour this solution over the herrings,
to cover them. Store the herrings in this 'pickle' and
use them, when needed. (The solution should be changed
periodically.)
Aberdaron, Lleyn.

The salted herrings were stored between layers of dry
salt in certain districts—it would not turn to brine the
second time, e.g.
Aber-porth, Cardiganshire.

Penwaig Hallt—Salted Herrings

salted herrings
potatoes in their jackets

Soak the salted herrings in cold water for three days
and three nights to remove excess salt.
Fill a saucepan with potatoes in their jackets (well
washed) and arrange the salted herrings in a layer on top.
Boil the potatoes, keeping the level of the water below
the herrings but allowing them to cook in the steam
around them.
Nefyn, Lleyn.

Salted herrings were generally served in this way in the
counties of north Wales and it made a popular dish for
dinner or supper during the winter months.

Sgadan Hallt—Salted Herrings

Roasting salted herrings was the most acceptable method
of cooking them in the counties of south Wales. The
general method was to roast them individually in front
of an open fire by means of a long toasting fork, but
in some districts in Cardiganshire and Carmarthenshire
they were placed on a special grilling frame known as
alch. This iron frame was suspended over an open fire
and the herrings, placed across the horizontal bars,
were allowed to cook slowly by direct heat. Roasted
herrings were served with bread and butter for tea or
supper.
Brynhoffnant, Cardiganshire.

In some districts, salted herrings were soaked in cold
water for a few days and then hung out to dry before
they were ready for cooking. A narrow rod, driven
through the eye-sockets of a dozen or so, would be
suspended from two nails at a convenient place outside
the house so that they dried in the heat from the sun.
Alternatively, they were hung inside the house in a
large, open chimney.

Cochi Penwaig—To Smoke Herrings

Clean and wash the herrings in the usual way and place
in layers, side by side, head to tail, in a large
earthenware bowl. Cover with salt and a little saltpetre
and leave overnight.
Light a fire of withered ash leaves and sprinkle a little
water over it to cause it to smoke. Hang the herrings
from a long rod above this fire and keep them in this
smoke for twenty four hours. (The fire was generally
lit in the outer-kitchen or out-house.)

Smoked herrings were generally roasted in front of an
open fire.
Llangybi, Caernarvonshire.

Mecryll mewn Saws—Mackerel in Sauce

two or three mackerel
three or four medium size onions
three tablespoonfuls white vinegar
one bay leaf
a little garlic
a little olive oil

Clean the mackerel and fry them well on both sides.
Fillet them, and remove all bones and skin.
Slice the onions and fry them in the oil together with
the garlic and bay leaf until brown. Allow them to cool
before adding the vinegar.
When cold, place the mackerel in a dish and pour the
sauce over them.

A delicious dish served for supper during the summer
months.
Cricieth, Caernarvonshire.

Pysgod Ffres o'r Afon—Freshwater Fish

In Wales, all freshwater fish were generally fried.
Salmon or sewin steaks or whole trout were fried in
bacon fat or butter and they were usually served for
dinner or supper. Yet, alternative methods of cooking
them were practised, as shown in the following selection
of recipes.

Go-ferwi Eog—Poached Salmon

salmon steak (approximately one pound)
milk
pepper and salt
bay leaf

Place the salmon steak and bay leaf in a saucepan,
cover with milk and season with salt and pepper.
Poach the salmon in the milk allowing fifteen minutes
for every pound weight. Alternatively, put the
ingredients in an earthenware dish and poach in a
moderately hot oven.
Slice the salmon steak and serve hot with parsley sauce,
or cold with bread and butter.
Llangrannog, Cardiganshire.

Ageru Eog (neu Wyniedyn)— Steamed Salmon or Sewin

salmon steak (approximately one pound)
pepper and salt
butter
water
fennel (or vinegar)

Using a double saucepan, put a few fennel leaves in the
lower one and fill it with water. Season the salmon
steak with pepper and salt, put a large knob of butter
on top and place in the second saucepan, over the lower
one. Boil the water and allow the salmon to cook in this
steam for about fifteen minutes.
Alternatively, place the salmon steak on a greased
enamel plate, rest it on top of a saucepan of boiling
water and cover it with the saucepan lid. Steam the
fish in this way, allowing fifteen minutes per pound
weight.
Steamed or poached salmon was highly commendable
for a person suffering from a stomach ailment.
Llandysul, Cardiganshire.

Berwi Eog (neu Wyniedyn)— Boiled Salmon or Sewin

fresh salmon steak (one or two pounds)
fennel
water
a little salt

Bring a saucepan of water to the boil, add the salt and
a few fennel leaves and then immerse the salmon steak
carefully in the water. Simmer gently, allowing fifteen
minutes for every pound, and taking care not to boil it
too briskly to prevent the salmon from flaking in the
water.
When cooked, drain well and slice, as needed. Serve
warm with parsley sauce or cold with salad and bread
and butter.
Cenarth, Carmarthenshire.

The gentry in the districts of Cenarth and Newcastle
Emlyn enjoyed the freshwater fish caught locally and
were fortunate in having better facilities for cooking
them. Informants who had been employed in these
mansions recall using a fish-kettle to boil the salmon or
sewin on the large range in the kitchen. When served
warm they would prepare parsley sauce or anchovy
sauce with salmon, and parsley sauce with sewin.

Berwi Eog mewn Llaeth— Salmon Boiled in Milk

salmon steak
salt
milk

Coracle-fishing on the river Teifi at Cenarth c. 1936

Immerse the salmon steak in boiling milk, add salt to taste and simmer gently, allowing about fifteen minutes for every pound in weight. Boiling it too briskly will cause the salmon to flake in the milk.

When cooked, drain and slice as needed. Serve warm with potatoes baked in their jackets or cold with fresh cream.

Cenarth, Carmarthenshire.

Eog a Winwns—Salmon and Onions

salmon steak (medium-sized)
one onion, sliced
bacon fat

Boil the salmon steak in salt water for about two minutes only. Drain well and remove all bone and skin. Flake the salmon and fry in bacon fat with the sliced onion.

Llandeilo'r-fân, Breconshire.

Cochi Eogiaid—To Smoke Salmon

In the past, experienced fishermen would smoke salmon during the winter months towards the beginning of the salmon season. This was the only method of preserving them at that time. The following method was practised by a fisherman from the Cenarth district, on the Carmarthenshire border.

Hang the salmon from its tail, split it open from the tail down to the head, remove the entrails and wash it thoroughly. Remove the bone found underneath the vent and fill that cavity with saltpetre. Keep the salmon open with a row of short skewers (approximately nine inches long). Treat about a dozen salmon in this way. Lay the salmon on their backs on a bed of salt in a stone or wooden trough, fill the open cavity with salt and keep all well covered with salt for a fortnight. Then remove them from the salt and wash them in fresh, running water (the old fishermen laid them in a shallow pool in the river for three days and three nights). When clean, hang them over a fire of withered oak

72

A typical Welsh farmhouse kitchen table, at which menservants sat at meal-times. >

leaves, allowing the smoke to whirl around them for three days and three nights. Usually, they would be hung by their tails from large nails driven into the open chimney stacks, with large branches of holly keeping them well away from the chimney wall. Store them in a convenient dry place, cut into steaks when needed and fry in butter.
Cenarth, Carmarthenshire.

Gwyniedyn—Sewin

one whole sewin (large)
thyme and parsley stuffing
bacon dripping

Clean the sewin in the usual way, and fill with thyme and parsley stuffing. Put it in an earthenware dish with a little bacon dripping and bake in a moderately hot oven.
Another favourite method of serving sewin in the Cenarth district was to cut it into steaks, fry them in butter and serve with boiled new potatoes and broad beans.
Cenarth, Carmarthenshire.

Rhostio Brithyllod—Baked Trout

three or four trout
salt
oatmeal
bacon dripping

Split and clean the trout and dry thoroughly. Remove the heads and tails, if desired.
Melt a little bacon dripping in an earthenware dish, or roasting tin, in the oven. Roll the trout in salted oatmeal, place them side by side on the melted fat and cover with greaseproof paper or lid. Bake in a moderately hot oven for about half an hour, remove the covering and allow them a further ten minutes to brown.

three or four trout
bacon dripping
a large onion or a few chives
a little warm water

Split and clean the trout and dry thoroughly. Remove the heads and tails if desired.

Place the trout, side by side, head to tail, in an earthenware dish or roasting tin and pour over them the bacon dripping dissolved in a little warm water. Slice the onion and place the rings on the trout. (Alternatively, use chopped chives in the same way.) Cover them with greaseproof paper or lid and bake in a moderately hot oven for about half an hour.
Remove the covering and allow them another ten minutes to brown.
Llandysul, Cardiganshire.

Saws Ffenigl—Fennel Sauce

two tablespoonfuls fennel leaves
half pint white sauce (unsweetened)

Wash the fennel leaves thoroughly, put them in boiling water and simmer until tender. (Do not overboil or they will turn into pulp.) Cool, strain and chop the leaves finely. Now add them to the prepared white sauce. Serve with hot salmon, sewin, or mackerel.
South Pembrokeshire.

Saws Anchovy—Anchovy Sauce

half a pint cold milk
pepper and salt
one tablespoonful plain flour
one teaspoonful anchovy essence

Follow the same method as given for *saws persli* but adding anchovy essence instead of parsley.
Serve with hot salmon.
Cenarth, Carmarthenshire.

Saws Cartref—Mayonnaise

yolks of two eggs
pinch of salt
half a teaspoonful dry mustard
half a teaspoonful sugar
one tablespoonful white vinegar (or wine vinegar)
approximately four tablespoonfuls salad oil
three or four tablespoonfuls cream

Place egg yolks, mustard, salt and sugar in a basin and beat lightly. Whisk in the salad oil and vinegar drop by drop so that it does not curdle. Mix thoroughly before adding the cream gradually. Again mix well.

Serve with cold crab or lobster with salad.
South Pembrokeshire.

Saws Persli—Parsley Sauce

half a pint cold milk
pepper and salt
one tablespoonful plain flour (or cornflour)
one tablespoonful finely chopped parsley

Blend the flour with a little of the milk. Heat the remainder of the milk in a saucepan and pour the flour mixture into it. Stir continuously with a wooden spoon and bring it to the boil. Add the parsley, season with pepper and salt and boil for a further two minutes.

Serve with hot salmon or sewin.
Cenarth, Carmarthenshire.

Saws Gwyn—White Sauce

half a pint cold milk
a pinch of salt
one dessertspoonful cornflour or plain flour
chives or parsley (finely chopped)

Follow the same method as given for *Saws Persli.*

This sauce was included in the *Pastai Gocos* (Cockle Pie), see page 68.
South Pembrokeshire.

Jams

Jam Cyrens Duon—Blackcurrant Jam

three pounds blackcurrants
three pints cold water
six pounds sugar

Pour the water over the fruit, bring to the boil and simmer
for fifteen minutes. Add the sugar, and boil for a further
ten minutes. Leave to cool and pour into warm pots.
Cover the jam immediately.
Pontyberem, Carmarthenshire.

Jam Riwbob—Rhubarb Jam

seven pounds rhubarb
seven pounds sugar cubes
the rind and juice of two lemons
two ounces almonds
six cloves
half a nutmeg } in a muslin bag

Cut the rhubarb into one-inch pieces, put in a large
saucepan and allow to stand in a warm place for a few
hours. (The hob alongside the open fire was such a
suitable place.) The heat will draw out the juice from
the rhubarb. To this liquid add the sugar, the almonds
(crushed), and the juice and grated rind of the lemons.
Boil until the mixture begins to thicken. Take away from
the heat and add the cloves and nutmeg in a muslin bag.
Allow this bag to remain in the jam while it cools in the
pan. When cool, remove the bag and pour the jam
into warm pots. Cover the pots in the usual way.
Pontyberem, Carmarthenshire.

Jam Mwyar Duon—Blackberry Jam

seven pounds blackberries
seven pounds sugar
one tablespoonful cold water

Put the blackberries in a large saucepan, add the cold
water and allow to stand over a very low heat for a few
hours. (The hob alongside the open fire was such a
suitable place.) Stir occasionally to help draw out the
juice from the fruit. When it is on the point of boiling,
add the sugar and boil briskly for three minutes only.
Leave to cool and then pour into warm pots.
Pontyberem, Carmarthenshire.

Jam Gwsberis—Gooseberry Jam

two pounds gooseberries
eight cupfuls cold water
seven pounds sugar

Pour the water over the gooseberries and boil for half an
hour. Add the sugar and boil for a further twenty
minutes. Leave to cool slightly before pouring it into
pots. Cover each pot while the jam is warm.
Pontyberem, Carmarthenshire.

Toffee

Cyflaith—Toffee

three pounds soft brown sugar
half a pound salted butter
juice of one lemon
quarter pint boiling water
(or a little more according to the consistency of the sugar)

Using an enamel or steel pan, gradually melt the sugar
in the boiling water over a low heat. Stir it continuously
with a wooden spoon until the sugar is thoroughly
melted. (This usually takes from twenty to thirty
minutes.) Remove the saucepan from the heat, add the
lemon juice and the softened butter, and stir into the
sugar. Boil this mixture fairly briskly for a further fifteen
minutes *without stirring it.*
Gently drop a teaspoonful of the mixture into a cupful of
cold water, and if it hardens at once it has reached the
required consistency. Pour the mixture slowly on to a
large, flat dish previously greased with butter. (Do not
scrape the pan clean as this mixture might turn the
toffee back into sugar.)
Butter the hands and 'pull' the toffee into long, golden
strands while hot. Cut into smaller pieces.
Pennant, Montgomeryshire.

Noson Gyflaith (Toffee Evening) was a traditional part of
Christmas or New Year festivities in some areas of north
Wales earlier this century. Families, in their turn, would
invite friends to their homes for supper, usually in the
form of a Christmas dinner, and it would be followed by
merriment, playing games, making toffee, and story
telling.

When the required ingredients had boiled to a certain
degree, the toffee was poured onto a well-greased slate
or stone slab. The hearth-stone itself was used for this
purpose in some houses. Members of the happy
gathering would then cover their hands with butter and
attempt to 'pull' the toffee while it was quite warm.
It was a skilled art to 'pull' and twist the toffee until it
became golden yellow in colour. Both the skilled and
unskilled would take part—the one being a source of
envy, the other a source of banter.

Toffee-making was also practised in parts of south
Wales, especially in the coal-mining areas. As far as we
know, it was not associated here with a particular
festive occasion, but housewives were known to sell it
from their homes or on local market stalls. It was known
by various names such as *taffi, dant,* or 'fanny', or
indeed it could be known by the name of the person
who made it, e.g. *losin Magws,* or *losin Ansin bach.*
Children would buy it—a six inch strip or two ounces
for a penny.

See frontispiece.

Cyflaith—Toffee

two pounds black treacle
two pounds golden syrup
two pounds granulated sugar
one pound butter

Put all the ingredients in a large saucepan (enamel or
copper) and melt slowly over a moderate heat. Then boil

the mixture briskly for about twenty minutes, stirring it continuously. Test its consistency at the end of the twenty minutes by dropping a teaspoonful of the boiling mixture into cold water. If it hardens at once leaving the water perfectly clear it has boiled to the required degree. Remove from the heat and pour the boiling toffee on to a stone slab or shallow dish, previously greased with butter.

Butter both hands and 'pull' the toffee into long golden strands while hot. Cut into smaller pieces before the toffee hardens.

Parc, Merioneth.

one pound black treacle
quarter pound butter
one pound brown sugar
one teaspoonful vinegar

Melt and boil the ingredients following the same method as given above and proceed to 'pull' the toffee into long strands.

Upper Banwy, Montgomeryshire.

Taffi a Ffani—Toffee and Fanny

one pound soft, brown sugar
one large cupful cold water
two teaspoonfuls vinegar
a knob of butter
oil of peppermint

Put all the ingredients (except for the oil of peppermint) in a cast iron saucepan over a moderate heat, and boil, stirring continuously, for fifteen minutes. Test a teaspoonful of the boiling mixture in cold water (see previous recipes) and if it hardens immediately remove the mixture from the heat.

Pour out the bulk of the mixture on to a greased slab or dish but retain a small amount in the saucepan. (Keep this in a warm place to prevent it from hardening.) Grease both hands with butter and 'pull' the toffee while it is hot, as quickly as possible, adding a few drops of the oil of peppermint while pulling. Continue pulling until a creamy colour is attained.

Place in long, flat strips, about an inch wide, on the table and pour the toffee that was retained to form a thin brown line along the centre of each strip.

Cut into smaller pieces before it hardens.

Gwaelod-y-garth, Glamorgan.

Drinks

Diod Fain—Small Beer

four pounds white sugar
one pound brown sugar
quarter pound root ginger
a handful of dandelion leaves
leaves from about five nettle stems
three gallons water
one and a half cupfuls liquid yeast
grated rind of one lemon and one orange

Wash all the leaves, cover them with the water and add all the other ingredients except for the sugar and yeast. Boil for about half an hour. Put the sugar in a large pan, strain the boiling liquid into it and dissolve. Then add two gallons of cold water to this mixture and leave to cool to blood heat before putting in the yeast. Cover the pan with a clean cloth and leave in a warm place overnight. Skim the surface on the following day and pour the beer into bottles. Cork securely.

This 'small beer' was a favourite drink with the south Wales coal-miner. He would look forward to having a glassful to quench his thirst as soon as he arrived home from the colliery and he and his family would also drink it with their Sunday lunch. Local demand proved profitable to many a widow who was anxious to augment her income. She would brew it weekly in large quantities to sell to regular customers for some two pence a bottle.
Aberdare, Glamorgan.

Diod Danadl Poethion—Nettle Beer

half a pound young nettle leaves
four ounces hops
half a pound sugar
one lemon, sliced
one ounce ginger
one ounce cream of tartar
a little yeast

Cover the leaves and hops with water and boil thoroughly. Strain the liquid and leave to cool to blood heat, before adding the remaining ingredients. Finally add a little yeast and allow to ferment overnight. Strain, pour into bottles and cork securely.

This drink was regarded as an excellent tonic.
Upper Banwy, Montgomeryshire.

Pop Danadl Poethion—Nettle Pop

one handful dandelion leaves
one handful nettle leaves
one handful ground ivy
one stick rhubarb
one and a half pounds sugar
half an ounce yeast

Cover the leaves and rhubarb with water and boil for ten minutes. Strain and add the sugar to the liquid. Allow to cool, then add the yeast and leave to ferment overnight. Strain again, pour into bottles and cork securely.
Gower Peninsula.

Sudd Danadl Poethion—Nettle Juice

young nettle leaves
water
sugar

Wash the leaves thoroughly and add a quart of water for every pound of leaves. Boil well for about one hour.
Strain and re-boil the liquid for half an hour, adding a pound of sugar for every pint.
Leave to cool before bottling.

This drink was taken as a tonic for purifying the blood.
Llandovery, Carmarthenshire.

Diod Cynhaeaf Gwair—Haytime Nectar

one gallon water
one pound raisins
two pounds sugar
the juice of three lemons

Boil the water and leave it to cool. Then add the raisins, the sugar and lemon juice and stir once daily for four days. Strain through muslin and pour into bottles. Cork securely at once.
Serve neat or diluted with hot water.
Gower Peninsula.

Diod Sinsir—Ginger Beer

one handful dandelion leaves
a few blackcurrant leaves
half a stick of rhubarb
a small lemon (sliced)
two quarts cold water
bruised root-ginger
one ounce yeast on a slice of bread
two pounds granulated sugar
one gallon boiling water

Put the leaves, the lemon and the ginger in the cold water and boil for half an hour. Strain the liquid into a large pan, add the boiling water to it and dissolve the sugar in it. Leave to cool to blood heat and then add the yeast. Allow to stand overnight, then strain and bottle.

A drink favoured by farmers during the hay harvest.
Llanarthney, Carmarthenshire.

Gwin Eirin Ysgawen—Elderberry Wine

four pints elderberries
one gallon cold water
three quarter pound sugar for every pint of liquid
two ounces yeast spread on toast
three ounces cloves (in a muslin bag)

Pour the cold water over the berries, bring to the boil and simmer for half an hour before adding the sugar and cloves. Boil again for a further fifteen minutes. Strain the liquid into an earthen pan and allow to cool to blood heat. Then add the yeast, spread on a piece of toast. Remove the toast on the following day and allow the wine to ferment for five days, removing the surface scum as needed. Then pour into bottles and cork loosely. The wine will continue to ferment and overflow so that it will be necessary to re-fill the bottles periodically. (Use the contents of one bottle to re-fill the others.) Cork securely in about a month's time when the fermentation has subsided.
Pontyberem, Carmarthenshire.

Siryp Ysgawen—Elderflower Syrup

elderflowers
water
sugar
ginger

Fill a large saucepan with elderflowers, cover with water and simmer for several hours. Strain the liquid and re-boil for half an hour. Add a little ground ginger and a pound of sugar for every pint of liquid. Boil again until the liquid thickens.
Pour into bottles when cool.

Dilute with hot water and take as an antidote for the common cold.
Upper Banwy, Montgomeryshire.

Shampein Eirin Ysgaw— Elderberry Champagne

ten pounds elderberries
eight pounds green grapes
six pounds damsons
fourteen pounds sugar
three ounces yeast spread on a thick slice of toast
four gallons boiling water

Put the elderberries, the green grapes (crushed) and the damsons in a large earthen pan and cover with the boiling water. Stir twice daily for fifteen days. Now pour through a strainer lined with muslin. Bring the strained liquid to the boil, remove from the heat immediately and then dissolve the sugar in it. (The liquid should *not* boil after adding the sugar.) Pour the liquid back into the earthen pan and allow to cool to blood heat before adding the yeast. Take out the toast on the following day and allow the wine to ferment for seven days, removing surface scum daily. Then pour it into bottles and cork loosely with rolls of paper. The wine will continue to ferment and overflow so that it will be necessary to re-fill the bottles periodically. (Use the contents of one bottle to re-fill the others.) Cork securely in about four to six weeks' time when the fermentation has subsided.
Pontyberem, Carmarthenshire.

Gwin Dant y Llew—Dandelion Wine

two quarts dandelion flowers
four quarts water
three oranges, sliced
three lemons, sliced
two pounds sugar cubes
half an ounce yeast spread over a piece of toast

Cover the flowers and the fruit with the water and boil for forty minutes. Then strain through muslin. Boil the liquid again for about half an hour and then add the sugar. Pour the liquid into a large pan and when cool add the yeast. Leave to ferment for three days. Strain, bottle and leave to mature for two months before using.
Nelson, Glamorgan.

Gwin Dant y Llew—Dandelion Wine

one gallon dandelion flowers
one orange
one lemon
approximately one inch root ginger
half an ounce yeast spread on a piece of toast
one gallon boiling water
three pounds sugar

Wash the flowers, put them in a large pan and cover with the boiling water. Leave to stand for three days, stirring frequently and crushing the flowers with a wooden spoon. Strain the liquid into a large saucepan, add the orange and lemon peel, cut into thin strips, the fruit itself, sliced thinly, the sugar and ginger.
Boil for half an hour. Leave to cool and then add the yeast. Allow the wine to ferment for six days.
Now strain, bottle and cork loosely. Cork securely in a month's time when bubbling has subsided.
Pontyberem, Carmarthenshire.

Gwin Mwyar Duon—Blackberry Wine

five pounds blackberries
one gallon cold water
one pound sugar to every quart of liquid
two ounces ginger
one ounce cloves

Put the fruit in an earthen pan and cover with the cold water. Stir once daily, for ten days, crushing the fruit with a wooden spoon. Pour the liquid into another pan through a fine sieve and then dissolve the sugar in it. Take a small quantity of this liquid, add the cloves and ginger to it, and boil for a few minutes. Allow this mixture to cool before adding it to the bulk in the pan. Leave to ferment for seven days, removing surface scum when necessary. Pour into bottles and cork loosely for the first month, then tightly when bubbling has subsided.
Pontyberem, Carmarthenshire.

Gwin Riwbob—Rhubarb Wine

five pounds rhubarb
one gallon cold water
one pound sugar for every quart of liquid
two ounces ginger
one ounce cloves

An example of the kitchen range, common in farmhouses and cottages throughout Wales in the early twentieth century. Tŷ Newydd Farm, Manod, near Blaenau Ffestiniog, Merioneth. >

Cut the rhubarb into one inch pieces and split. Put them in an earthen bowl and cover with the cold water. Stir daily for ten days, crushing the fruit with a wooden spoon. Pour the liquid into another bowl through a fine sieve and then dissolve the sugar in it. Take a small quantity of this liquid, add the ginger and cloves to it and boil for a few minutes. Leave this mixture to cool before pouring it back into the bulk in the bowl.

Leave to ferment for seven days, removing surface scum when necessary.

Pour the wine into bottles, cork loosely for the first month, then tightly when bubbling has subsided.
Pontyberem, Carmarthenshire.

Medd—Mead

one ounce dried hops
four pounds honey (freshly extracted from the comb)
two gallons water
one ounce yeast spread on a piece of toast

Pour the water over the honey and the hops, and boil slowly for an hour. Then strain into a pan and leave to cool before adding the yeast. Take out the toast on the following morning and stir the liquid well. Cover the pan with a clean cloth and leave for five days. Strain and pour into bottles but do not cork securely until bubbling has ceased.

The mead should be allowed one year to mature before using.
Llanfachraeth, Anglesey.

Medd—Mead

honey combs
sugar
ground ginger
water

After extracting all the honey, immerse the combs in a panful of cold water and leave to soak for a day or two. Strain the liquid and boil for half an hour, then dissolve the sugar in it (approximately one pound to every gallon of liquid). When cool, pour into earthen bottles and keep for a few weeks before using.

The mead was usually prepared in early autumn so that it had time to mature before Christmas.
Gower Peninsula.

Index

Cooking Temperatures

Oven Description	Electric Oven Setting	Gas Oven Setting
Cool	300°F. (149°C.)	1.2
Warm	325°F. (163°C.)	3
Moderate	350°F. (177°C.)	4
Fairly hot	375°F. (191°C.)	5
	400°F. (204°C.)	6
Hot	425°F. (218°C.)	7

Weights and Measures

Weights

Imperial	Metric
$\frac{1}{4}$ ounce	7.09g
$\frac{1}{2}$ ounce	14.17g
1 ounce	28.35g
$\frac{1}{4}$ pound	113.04g
$\frac{1}{2}$ pound	227.00g
1 pound	454.00g
2 pounds	907.00g
3 pounds	1361.00g

Liquids

1 liquid ounce	28.4 ml.
$\frac{1}{4}$ pint	142.0 ml.
$\frac{1}{2}$ pint	284.0 ml.
1 pint	568.0 ml.
1 quart	1137.0 ml.